Part 1
Ground Zero

Moving from
Shattered to Strong

THE FOUNDATIONS OF RECOVERY

From Sexual Addiction And Intimacy Avoidance For Christians

Matt Burton
Kevin Rose
Laura Burton

Part 1
Ground Zero

Moving from
Shattered to Strong

THE FOUNDATIONS OF RECOVERY

From Sexual Addiction
And Intimacy Avoidance
For Christians

**MATT BURTON
KEVIN ROSE
LAURA BURTON**

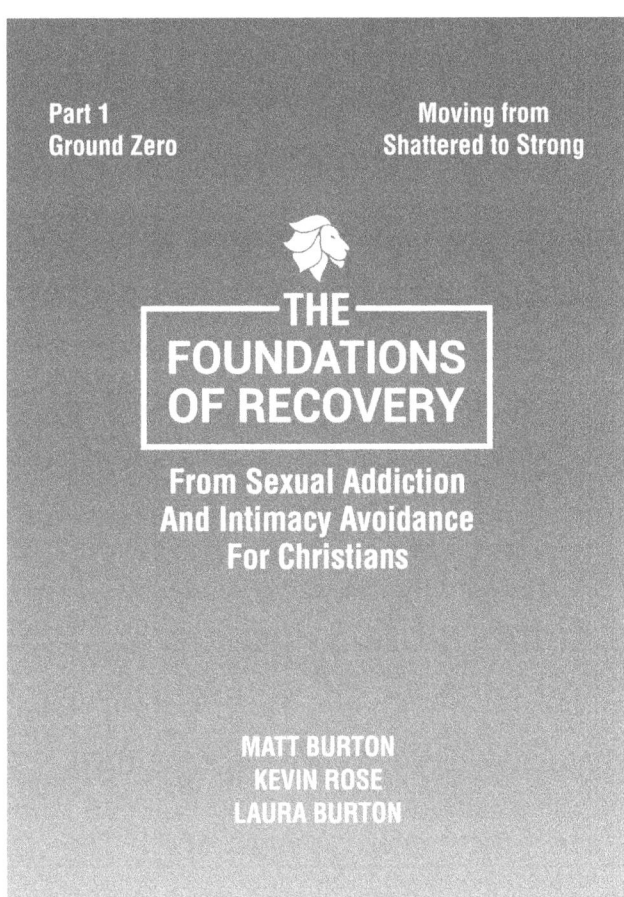

Copyright © 2025 by Becoming Well, LLC

All rights reserved. No part of this book may be reproduced or transmitted in any form, or by any means, electronic or mechanical, including photocopying, recording, or by information storage or retrieval systems, without permission in writing from the copyright owner.

The views and opinions expressed in this book are those of the author and do not necessarily reflect the official policy or position of Becoming Well, LLC

Published by Becoming Well, LLC

www.BecomingWellInstitute.com

Library of Congress Control Number

Paperback ISBN: 979-8-3493-8583-4

E-book ISBN: 979-8-3493-8584-1

Cover design by Monira

Printed in the United States of America

Table of Contents

Recovery Tool Box 3
1. Exercise Book 4
2. 3 Goals 5
3. Meetings 7
4. Phone Calls 9
5. 90 in 90 11
6. Choose a Sponsor 13
7. 30-Day Checklist 15
8. Weekly Check-in 17
9. 24-Hour Tell Policy 19
10. 100% Responsible 20
11. Rubber Band 21
12. Blockers and Accountability Software 23
13. Book Work 25
14. HALT BS 27
15. Gratitude List 29
16. Bookending 31

12 Steps in a Year 33
17. Step 1 35
18. Step 2 37
19. Step 3 39
20. Step 4 41
21. Step 5 43
22. Step 6 45
23. Step 7 47
24. Step 8 49
25. Step 9 51
26. Step 10 53
27. Step 11 55
28. Step 12 57

Helping My Partner Heal (Part 1) — 59
29. Rebuilding Trust Pyramid – Honesty — 61
30. Rebuilding Trust Pyramid – Safety — 63
31. Rebuilding Trust Pyramid – Consistency — 65
32. Rebuilding Trust Pyramid – Intimacy — 67
33. Standing Shoulder to Shoulder — 69
34. Demeanor - Part 1 — 73
35. 70/30 to 80/20 — 75
36. Stabilization — 76
37. Emptying the Pain Closet — 79
38. Empathy Exercise — 81
39. No Defend Challenge – 13 Weeks — 85
40. Daily Check In — 87
41. Feeling Wheel — 91
42. Most Flawed Moment — 93

Maintain a Sobriety Focus — 95
43. Staying Sober Checklist — 97
44. 3 Circles — 99
45. SA/PA Lapse and Relapse Worksheet — 101
46. Appreciation and Resignation Letters for SA/PA/Infidelity — 103
47. SA/PA Relapse Chain — 107
48. SA/PA Relapse Prevention Plan — 109
49. Top 5 Intimacy Avoidance — 111
50. Intimacy Avoidance – Appreciation and Resignation Letters — 113
51. IA Relapse Chain — 125
52. IA Relapse Prevention Plan — 126

Addendum — 131

40 ways to be IA (Intimacy Avoidant) — 139

Workgroups and Intensives — 145

Books and Courses — 153

AUTHORS' NOTE

Although the publisher and the authors have made every effort to ensure that the information in this book was correct at press time, and while this publication is designed to provide accurate information regarding the subject matter covered, the publisher and the authors assume no responsibility for errors, inaccuracies, omissions, or any other inconsistencies herein and hereby disclaim any liability to any party for any loss, damage, or disruption caused by errors or omissions, whether such errors or omissions result from negligence, accident, or any other cause.

This publication is meant as a source of valuable information for the reader. However, it is not meant as a substitute for direct expert assistance. If such a level of assistance is required, the services of a competent professional should be sought.

MATT AND LAURA BURTON
www.BecomingWellInstitute.com

INTRODUCTION

Welcome to Foundations of Recovery. Regardless of where you're at on your recovery journey, this workbook will help you chart a path of health. It will also benefit those hurt by your destructive behaviors and the ways of thinking connected to them. In short, *Foundations of Recovery* will help you get better.

This workbook was birthed out of 30-plus years of personal recovery and walking with thousands of men through their recovery journeys. Whether you are working on *Foundations of Recovery – Part 1: Ground Zero*, or *Foundations of Recovery – Part 2: Digging Deeper*, you will find that the exercises in this workbook will expand the depth of your recovery. It will also provide you with many, many tools to help you navigate and succeed in your individual and relational recovery.

Foundations of Recovery – Part 1: Ground Zero focuses on expanding your recovery toolbox, getting through the 12 steps in a year, and doing exercises around helping your partner heal, as well as maintaining a sobriety focus.

Foundations of Recovery – Part 2: Digging Deeper focuses on whether you are "all in" with regards to recovery, how to understand the destructiveness of lying and exercises to combat it, how objectification is so destructive, and how to change object thinking. It also offers a focus on helping your partner heal. You will be educated on the warning signs of potential relapse and given the tools you need to journey long-term through the marathon that is recovery.

Each workbook contains 52 exercises. We hope you will complete at least one exercise per week and finish this workbook in one year. For those wishing to accelerate their recovery, you will complete two exercises per week: one in *Foundations of Recovery – Part 1: Ground Zero*, and one in *Foundations of Recovery – Part 2: Digging Deeper*. Do this and you'll complete both workbooks in a year. Whether you get them done in one or two years, these workbooks, when done weekly and shared with your partner, will help you profoundly in your individual and relational recovery journey.

Other materials available through Becoming Well, LLC and our Becoming Well Institute here in Tucson, AZ may be helpful in your journey. They are listed in the appendix of this book with a full list on our website. Virtual sessions for individuals and couples, Recovery Workgroups, Couples Private Intensives, Couples Group Intensives, Wounded Partner Healing Intensives, Men's Recovery Intensives, and Men's Going Deeper Healing Intensives, as well as courses, books, and videos are also available worldwide.

Please contact us for further information.

You can visit our website at

www.BecomingWellInstitute.com

for access other resources for you and your partner

Becoming Well, LLC and Becoming Well Institute

Phone number: 520-355-5322

Email address: Info@MyBecomingWell.com

Recovery Tool Box

THE FOUNDATIONS OF RECOVERY - PART 1 GROUND ZERO

 Exercise 1 **Exercise Book**

Completed in a Year

Between the two exercise books (*Foundations of Recovery – Part 1: Ground Zero* and *Part 2: Digging Deeper*), you will have 104 total exercises to complete over the next two years. Doing the math, this means 1 exercise per week. Pairing this expectation with the **Daily Times for Recovery**, you will be on track to complete them all. *Be aware that if you're in a Becoming Well Workgroup, you will have planned exercises (homework) to complete and discuss while in group 2-3 times monthly. This counts towards your expectation of 1 exercise per week.

Why do you have this expectation for yourself? Part of your growth in recovery, whether you are in a relationship or not, is creating habits of daily recovery for the rest of your life. Like your physical body, your heart and spirit need exercise to remain healthy. If you don't stay in recovery, you will drift out of health.

Think of a healthy habit you have developed in your life. How has it benefited you?

If you haven't kept up with the habit listed above, what did you begin to lose?

2 Timothy 2:15 RSV

Do your best to present yourself to God as one approved, a workman who has no need to be ashamed, rightly handling the word of truth.

Father, there is power in consistency. I remember that it is Your approval that I need in this life. I will be diligent in reading the scriptures, recording my progress, and applying Your principles into my everyday life. Thank You for the many blessings I will reap because of this decision. In Jesus' name, Amen.

If you are ready to commit to this practice, this is great news! Share it with a recovery partner in a workgroup and a sponsor. I, _____(name), say _____(yes/no), I will commit to completing one exercise per week during my **Daily Times for Recovery**.

Steps 1-3 Connection: When we come together to recover, we do so with the power of accountability. Share your commitment with another person.
How does it feel to be in community with others who are also seeking health?
On a recovery call, ask someone what this commitment has produced for them. Record their answer here.

PARTNER CONNECT Share your commitment to complete the 52 exercises with your partner. Who are you going to choose as an accountability partner to help hold you to this commitment?

RECOVERY TOOL BOX

3 Goals

Exercise 2

If you don't have a goal, you're not going to reach it. In individual recovery and relational recovery, it's vital to make sure that you have goals that you both write out and periodically check to make sure that you are executing them well.

That's where 3 & 3 come in:
- ☐ 3 individual recovery goals
- ☐ 3 relationship recovery goals.

These are 12-month goals. You're going to write out three individual recovery goals. Make these for yourself, for your SA recovery, and for your IA recovery.

1.

2.

3.

Hebrews 5: 14 AMP

But solid food is for the [spiritually] mature, whose senses are trained by practice to distinguish between what is morally good and what is evil.

Father, Your word establishes my moral boundaries. I will obey Your precepts so I can create godly boundaries in my moral life. As I practice keeping inside Your boundary lines, I will be able to distinguish even more clearly other aspects of my moral life that need to be dealt with and continue to hone myself in practicing what is good and holy in Your sight. In Jesus' name, Amen.

Next, you're going to write out relationship recovery goals. Again, do these independent of your partner. Make it come from your heart and your desires for your partnership.

1.

2.

3.

Share your relational goals with your partner. In these beginning stages of recovery, whatever their feelings may be about your goals, practice the **Empathy Exercise** regarding their feelings. Reflect here on your partner's feelings and how they are understandable in this stage of recovery.

Feeling: _____ Why it's understandable…

Feeling: _____ Why it's understandable…

Step 1 Connection: The powerlessness of this step is also designed to have you reflect on what *is* in your power. In a calendar one year from now, whether digitally in your device or on a hardcopy calendar, set a reminder to reflect on your 3 & 3.

PARTNER CONNECT Share your goals with your partner.

RECOVERY TOOL BOX

Meetings

Exercise 3

Do you remember the feeling you had when you first joined a Becoming Well Workgroup OR other recovery meeting? Maybe it caught you off guard, that people would come together to support each other. There is a safety that meetings provide, which cannot be found elsewhere.

When you share the reasons why you joined a recovery group, that darkest moment, that thing you thought you'd never share, you become freer. You begin recovering right there!

In a Becoming Well weekly meeting, you will be fully accepted while being fully known. Historically, many recovery groups offer this type of environment and expectation while maintaining confidentiality. Please see appendix____, where you can explore additional meetings to attend throughout the week in case you need them (e.g., workaholics anonymous, sexaholics anonymous, overeaters anonymous, etc.).

What brought you into Becoming Well meetings and how did it feel to share, be open, and be honest?

What do you gain from sharing openly and honestly with others?

When you are fully accepted and known by God, how do you feel?

Why?

Hebrews 10:25 MEV

Let us not forsake the assembling of ourselves, as is the manner of some, but let us exhort one another, especially as you see the day approaching.

Father, I will keep my word and be diligent in attending all of my meetings. It is an honor to be a part of this circle where I will be fully accepted and fully known. I know that You are in our midst as we share and do the work necessary for recovery. I thank You for it. In Jesus' name, Amen.

Step 2 Connection: Explain how members in your meetings have displayed the character of God to you.

[   ]

PARTNER CONNECT Although you shouldn't share any specifics about what goes on in your confidential meetings, be sure to share the time and day of your meeting with your partner. Also, at the end of each meeting, note what you learned about yourself during that time. Share this with your partner every week, as it will help them trust you more if they understand that you are learning and growing.

Phone Calls

Exercise 4

Recovery is done together. We sharpen each other, accept each other, and praise one another throughout our battle with negative thinking, sexual struggle, moral failure, and unhealthy relationship habits with our partners. We choose to make a phone call for several different reasons. Here are some:

Reasons for Making a Phone Call

Welcome others into recovery * Share your story * Share burdens of recovery

Receive feedback * Process a Becoming Well Exercise * Ask questions about a Step

Process a negative thought about a partner * Process a temptation to act out sexually

Practice exercises for relational growth

Bookend the days/events/travel/situations when we know we will be tempted to avoid or act out

The goal is to make at least 6 calls each week. It's important to grow relationships during recovery. Isolation and secrets have broken down what we would want, which is a fulfilling life.

How have isolation and secrets hurt you and your relationships?

Who are you able to talk with about your recovery?

Make a list of trusted confidential people you can call, and write what makes them a safe person to talk with.

1.
2.
3.
4.
5.
6.
7.

Proverbs 1:5 AMP

The wise will hear and increase their learning, and a person of understanding will acquire wise counsel and the skill [to steer his course wisely and lead others to the truth] ...

Father, I understand the wisdom in seeking guidance and counsel from my accountability partners and leaders. It keeps me honest and on the path of righteousness. This is my true desire. Thank You for connecting me with such caring and godly men. In Jesus' name, Amen.

Step (All) Connection: All of the steps have the word "we" in them.

Why is it beneficial for you to invest your time in making recovery phone calls?

[ ]

PARTNER CONNECT Share your answer to the question "how have isolation and secrets hurt you and your relationship?" with your partner. Have a discussion about how they see it.

RECOVERY TOOL BOX

90 in 90

Exercise 5

This exercise is particularly useful for those looking to recover from addiction.

Because intimacy avoidance is not considered an addiction but a way of thinking or state of mind, we are talking about 90 meetings in 90 days for those individuals looking to break free from the chains of sex addiction.

Alcoholics Anonymous (AA) coined the saying "It works if you work it," but how do you work recovery? Other than using this exercise book, you can go to meetings to form relationships with others in recovery. Meetings can help you heal from the shame of your sexual acting out, past and present.

"SA.org" and "Next Meeting for SA" are two locations online to join a meeting. You can be on the phone or video call within seconds. Listening to and sharing with a community that wants the same goal – freedom from lust and sexual addiction – is a tremendous help. The more support you have in the fight, the better. The fact is, people around the world are struggling and you are not alone. This collective community can also be found at local churches, Celebrate Recovery, Regeneration, and, of course, a Becoming Well Workgroup.

For your brain, sex is like a drug, stronger than heroin. That's why 3 months (90 days) is recommended to begin your sex addiction recovery with traction and in community.

Track your 90 meetings below

1	2	3	4	5	6	7	8	9	10
11	12	13	14	15	16	17	18	19	20
21	22	23	24	25	26	27	28	29	30
31	32	33	34	35	36	37	38	39	40
41	42	43	44	45	46	47	48	49	50
51	52	53	54	55	56	57	58	59	60
61	62	63	64	65	66	67	68	69	70
71	72	73	74	75	76	77	78	79	80
81	82	83	84	85	86	87	88	89	90

If you are willing to use this exercise, summarize what you will gain from attending meetings.

Steps 1-3 Connection: Write a recovery prayer, admitting your powerlessness over sexual temptation to God. Express your belief that He can win the battle, and open your heart for His will for your life.

Colossians 3:23 AMP

Whatever you do [whatever your task may be], work from the soul [that is, putting your very best effort] as [something done] for the Lord and not for men...

Father, I throw my entire being into completing this task of 90 in 90. Thank You for blessing my efforts and setting me free! In Jesus' name, Amen.

THE FOUNDATIONS OF RECOVERY - PART 1 GROUND ZERO

PARTNER CONNECT

If you have committed to attend 90 meetings in 90 days, share this fact with your partner.

RECOVERY TOOL BOX

Choose a Sponsor   Exercise 6

When you join a Becoming Well Workgroup OR recovery group, you will be meeting guys who are also recovering from sexual addiction, infidelity/betrayal, intimacy avoidance, or a combination of these. In this process of becoming honest, open, and vulnerable, you will be required to make phone calls as part of your weekly routine. This is where you need to start looking for your sponsor.

After you connect over the phone or video call, ask yourself: do they have experience in recovery, have they gone through similar struggles as me, and where are they at in mending and rebuilding trust with their partner?

Choosing a sponsor is an individual choice, and it's an important one. Your sponsor will be the first person you reach out to if you are in a negative mindset, tempted to act out in SA, or need someone to *Bookend* with. Of course, you will need to have more than one person to call in case your sponsor is unavailable.

Since joining your workgroup, who have you connected with? In what ways are you similar?

How will you benefit from having a sponsor?

Why would a call with a sponsor help you grow and recover?

Hebrews 13:17 MEV

Obey your leaders and submit to them, for they watch over your souls as those who must give an account. Let them do this with joy and not complaining, for that would not be profitable to you.

Father, thank You for bringing leaders and counselors into my life who sincerely care for me and my partner. Help me to remain humble and to follow their directions and advice. This will guarantee our success and put us on the right path. In Jesus' name, Amen.

Choose! Ask a member of your workgroup to sponsor you in Becoming Well. Write why you chose them below.

Name_____

I chose them because...

Step 1 Connection: Explain how the concept of "We" is demonstrated in having a sponsor to support you.

PARTNER CONNECT Once you have chosen a sponsor, share that fact with your partner. You may share the first name of your sponsor with your partner as well as tell them the reason(s) you chose this particular person. Be careful that you don't divulge any private information about your sponsor to your partner.

Romans 14:12 ISV Consequently, each one of us will give an account of himself to God. Father, I am determined to walk circumspectly knowing that You are watching my every movement. I will keep record of my progress with the confidence that You are giving me the grace necessary to be victorious in my moral conduct. In Jesus' name, Amen.

RECOVERY TOOL BOX

30-Day Checklist

Exercise 7

Use this template to keep track of your recovery goals. The Appendix can direct you to the exercises that correspond to each column. P1/P2 = Exercise found in corresponding workbook, Part 1 or 2

Day	Daily Prayers	Daily Check In (P1)	Empathy Exercise (P1)	Gratitude List (P1)	Exercises (P1 or P2)	Phone Call (P1)	Cynical Script (P2)	Played Victim Y/N	Defend/ Explain (P1)	SA Relapse Y/N (P1)	IA Behavior Y/N (P1)	Lie Y/N (P2)
1												
2												
3												
4												
5												
6												
7												
8												
9												
10												
11												
12												
13												
14												
15												
16												
17												
18												
19												
20												
21												
22												
23												
24												
25												
26												
27												
28												
29												
30												

RECOVERY TOOL BOX

Weekly Check-in   Exercise 8

The weekly check-in is based on 4 areas of recovery that must be given attention.

In your Becoming Well Workgroup, you will be reading through key questions to stay accountable and listen to others. Reflect on how you can give feedback in the form of a **praise** and a **sharpen**.

The Check-in has the following sections:

1. Sobriety	This includes reporting sobriety and whether you are following the program's suggested tools for recovery. Here we recognize that the destruction from our addiction (SA) or ways of thinking/operating (IA) will destroy our relationships if we are not held accountable to others.
2. Relational Work	We report to our partners, asking them for feedback about how we are doing this week. This is an essential part of studying and learning about our partners. We strive to practice empathy, cease being defensive, and be honest with our partners to build trust. Additionally, you will report to the group how your partner rated the relationship and why. This is meant to help you draw closer to a state of connection and commitment with your partner.
3. Group Work	The group work section of the check-in is an accountability section that has you track the number of recovery phone calls and your daily practice of gratitude. We attend weekly groups to show consistency in our commitment to recovery. This is also a trust builder with our partners.
4. Book Work	Here is where you report on how often you have done step work or workbook exercises during the week. This section of accountability coincides with our recovery plan created in your *Daily Times for Recovery* exercise. If you make the time, it will be evident week to week.
5. Highs and Lows	In the final part of our check-in, we are given time to share the past week's most flawed and successful moments in our recovery and relationship.
*You must express being "open to feedback" or "not open to feedback" at the end of every check-in	
Feedback	**Praise** When listening to a check-in, be prepared to encourage each other **Sharpen** Depending on where someone is struggling, give a suggestion or rhetorical question for someone to consider

If you are looking to join a *Becoming Well Work Group,* why wait?

All Steps Connection: Read over all the steps.

Name 3 steps for which you will need a workgroup community to help you recover and why.

1. Step____Why…

2. Step____Why…

3. Step____Why…

<u>**PARTNER CONNECT**</u> In addition to completing your Weekly Check In for group, you also need to read it to your partner and ask for their input. This should be done every week, preferably the day before your meeting. If you have an evening meeting, and it is ok with your partner, you can go through it with them that morning. Do not wait until the last minute and then claim that your partner didn't have time or didn't want to do it. The Weekly Check In is your responsibility, and you are responsible for making sure that you create a safe environment that your partner wants to participate in.

Galatians 6:1-3 MSG

Live creatively, friends. If someone falls into sin, forgivingly restore him, saving your critical comments for yourself. You might be needing forgiveness before the day's out. Stoop out and reach out to those who are oppressed. Share their burdens, and so complete Christ's law.

Father, Your word is clear that we are to be accountable to each other. Grace me with humility to make godly choices and not feed illicit desires so I can honestly give a good report to my group. Help me to be understanding of others and to encourage them to choose good. I will also praise others when they experience victory. Their sorrow is my sorrow, and their victory is my victory. You created us to be victorious in every circumstance and I bless You for it! In Jesus' name, Amen.

RECOVERY TOOL BOX

24-Hour Tell Policy   Exercise 9

To build trust and maintain accountability, it is your responsibility to have a 24-hour tell policy and honor it. The policy must include any behavior that would be considered as acting out in your struggle or breaking trust with regard to what you have agreed to follow through with for the relationship, family, or partner.

If you break your sobriety from SA or cross any boundary, it is important to tell your partner as soon as possible. New trauma may ensue by keeping the truth from your partner, so it is best to tell them. In your mind, it may seem like you're saving them from pain by not telling them, but that is a lie. Secrets about our struggle will only hurt you and them in the long run. It is selfish to keep the truth from them.

Processing how you will tell your partner beforehand is wise. Also, by anticipating any feelings they may have, you can prepare to *Hear and Validate* your partner.

What boundaries are included in your 24-Hour Tell Policy?

Agree with your partner about each area listed.

How do you think your partner would feel if you didn't tell them when you broke the policy? What is at stake?

Psalm 32:3 MSG When I kept it all inside, my bones turned to powder, my words became daylong groans.

Father, give me the courage to admit my faults to my wounded partner. I am asking for wisdom as to how to disclose my failure in keeping my commitments in a way that will not traumatize them. Thank You for Your mercy and help me not to fall again. In Jesus' name, Amen.

On a phone call with another person in recovery, discuss each other's policies. What's the same/different?

Step 3 Connection: How has "your will" been destructive when it comes to hiding behaviors?

<u>PARTNER CONNECT</u> Complete this exercise with your partner. Be sure they are aware of the 24-Hour Tell Policy. Ask them what they do and do not want to know and take notes.

Exercise 10 — 100% Responsible

Blaming someone or something else for your behavior will stop you from healing and recovering. Being 100% responsible means that you take the weight of what your actions have done. Realize that feeling guilty is natural as you get started on your recovery. Avoiding your responsibility to your partner has caused pain and been destructive to the relationship.

You then have a choice: to feel sorry for yourself, or to move forward into actions that will help you recover. Your partner cannot take responsibility for you. Focusing on yourself and what you need to take responsibility for is the foundation of recovery.

Ask yourself, "Am I 100% responsible for the devastation I've caused and my recovery from it?" Yes___ No___

Recall a time when you avoided responsibility. How did your choice cause pain for others?

> **Galatians 6:5 AMP** For every person will have to bear [with patience] his own burden [of faults and shortcomings for which he alone is responsible].
>
> Father, I alone am 100% responsible for my conduct and actions. I will not shift blame or make excuses. Give me mercy and strength to be forthright and strong in You. In Jesus' name, Amen.

Your partner wants to feel safe.

How is taking responsibility related to building safety for them?

Say, "I am 100% responsible and I can recover!" 5 times. Do you believe it? Why or why not?

Step 3 Connection: Write a recovery prayer, thanking God for His will and strength to take responsibility.

PARTNER CONNECT Ask your partner for their input on how taking responsibility is related to them feeling safe. Write down what they say in the space provided (item 2 of the exercise).

RECOVERY TOOL BOX

Rubber Band   Exercise 11

"Snapping out of Destructive Thoughts and Behaviors"

The rubber band is a positive punishment tool. It's adding something unpleasant to discourage unwanted behavior. It's retraining your brain.

For sex addiction, the snap of the rubber band would be for behaviors such as fantasizing, ogling (checking out), or any form of lust. This is very powerful when you follow the snap with the exercise *Pray to Humanize.* By treating those we objectify like humans we are no longer able to objectify them in that moment.

For intimacy avoidance, the snap of the rubber band would be for any cynical script your mind goes to about your partner. To combat this negative story about your partner, follow the rubber band snap with a praise about your partner from your *Gratitude List*.

The rubber band brings mindfulness about your behaviors. It reminds you how destructive your behavior is and how the behavior is not good for you. Diligent use of the rubber band is essential. Snapping immediately is the key to using the rubber band effectively. It sends the message to your brain that what you just thought is unhealthy, destructive thinking.

Be aware that snapping the rubber band in front of your partner can create unnecessary anxiety for them because they don't know why you snapped the rubber band. The *presence* of the rubber band, however, sends the message to your partner that you're serious about your recovery.

Why are you willing to commit to wearing the rubber band?

Record the date you began wearing it.

Date___/___/___

My why is…

Write down as many situations as you can predict where you will need to snap your rubber band. (SA or IA)

1.
2.
3.
4.
5.
6.
7.

Proverbs 10: 17 AMP He who learns from instruction and correction is on the [right] path of life [and for others his example is a path toward wisdom and blessing], but he who ignores and refuses correction goes off course [and for others his example is a path toward sin and ruin].

Father, I am using wisdom to redirect my thinking and retrain my brain to recognize evil. I will now meditate on wholesome thoughts. I will be diligent in practicing godliness and You will bless my efforts according to Your word. In Jesus' name, Amen.

THE FOUNDATIONS OF RECOVERY - PART 1 GROUND ZERO

Step 1 Connection: How is the rubber band connected to you being powerless over your struggle?

<u>**PARTNER CONNECT**</u> Explain the reason behind wearing a rubber band to your partner. Ask them if they'd prefer not to see you snap it or if they're okay with it. If they're okay with it, don't hide the use of your rubber band from them.

Blockers and Accountability Software

Exercise 12

There are many options for software and blockers. First, realize there is a difference between the two.

Blockers monitor activity and stop access to websites and apps that can be used to fuel sexual addiction. Software puts high accountability on the person in recovery because they know that all their activity is monitored.

We recommend choosing accountability software and an accountability partner who will receive notifications by text or email of your activity.

Common Software Used: Covenant Eyes, Accountable2You, and Ever Accountable

Common Accountability Partner Options: Pastor, Close Friend, Sponsor, or Spouse/Partner

*Partners may not want to be your SA accountability partner

The key is that your accountability partner must actually hold you to your commitment and be willing to ask the hard questions about what led you to your acting-out behavior in the first place. Accountability software serves as a door for deeper understanding of your addiction in the case of a relapse.

What is the purpose of accountability software for all your devices?

How will you and your partner grow closer if you added this layer of accountability to your SA recovery?

Step 1 Connection: How is accountability software related to accepting that you're powerless over your SA?

PARTNER CONNECT Talk to your partner about your blockers and/or accountability software. In addition to your sponsor or recovery partner, ask your partner if they want to be added to the list of who sees your reports. If they don't, offer to ask your recovery partner or sponsor if they would be comfortable sharing your breaks in sobriety with your partner, should you dishonor your 24-hour tell policy.

Romans 2: 5-8 MSG You are not getting away with anything. every refusal and avoidance of God adds fuel to the fire. The day is coming when it's going to blaze hot and high, God's fiery and righteous judgement. Make no mistake: In the end you get what's coming to you - Real Life for those who work on God's side, but to those who insist on getting their own way and take the path of least resistance, Fire!

Father, I repent of the attitude that I got away with sin. I didn't get away with anything! I rotted my brain, destroyed my conscience, and violated my wounded partner and family. When I am online, I choose to be held accountable with my thoughts and emotions, and my actions will follow. I declare that I am DEAD to SIN and ALIVE to CHRIST! I will do everything in my power to resist evil. Thank You in advance for the strength and determination to honor You, myself, my wounded partner, and my family. In Jesus' name, Amen.

RECOVERY TOOL BOX

Book Work

Exercise 13

We either make the time or we don't. Your recovery is going to take deliberate planning and actions to recover from years or even decades of Sexual Addiction and/or Intimacy Avoidance. This needs to be a daily commitment because, if your mind is set on recovery every day, then your actions towards your partner, family, friends, and yourself will begin to change.

You need to put in a small amount of time every day. Below is a week-by-week planner for when you can set aside time, and how much. Creating this and sharing it with your partner will show them how serious you are about recovery. It will give both of you a way to measure that seriousness.

For the partner, this is one of many ways you can rebuild trust. Maybe they have never seen you follow through on your recovery. Maybe they have only seen half efforts and half-truths from you, which has demonstrated a lack of commitment to recovery. Time is a factor that can communicate how hard you truly want to work. So make it a significant amount of time, around 20 minutes at least.

Next, what are you working on? The rhythm you want to have is based on what you are recovering from. This is the rule of 3 and 3. Day 1, read recovery book (SA/IA). Day 2, Exercise from this book. Day 3, step book around SA/IA recovery. Then repeat again for Day 4, 5 & 6. **Expectation 6/7 days of recovery.**

Rhythm: Book, Work book, Step book; Book, Work book, Step book, Day off.

Day	Time: From	Time: To	What I plan to work on
Monday			
Tuesday			
Wednesday			
Thursday			
Friday			
Saturday			
Sunday			

> **2 Timothy 2:15 RSV** Do your best to present yourself to God as one approved, a workman who has no need to be ashamed, rightly handling the word of truth.
>
> Father, there is power in consistency. I remember that it is Your approval that I need in this life. I will be diligent in reading the scriptures, recording my progress, and applying Your principles into my everyday life. Thank You for the many blessings I will reap because of this decision. In Jesus' name, Amen.

Step 1 Connection: Have you ever been able to manage a day-to-day routine for self-improvement and devotion to address your own brokenness? If so, how can you empower yourself to commit to a daily plan? What's at stake? If you haven't, then what is motivating you towards recovery and commitment to a daily plan?

THE FOUNDATIONS OF RECOVERY - PART 1 GROUND ZERO

PARTNER CONNECT Once you have completed your plan of action, share this with your partner for extra accountability. Remember, following through on your plan is a way to build trust with your partner. But beware: a lack of follow-through on your part will lead to more distrust!

HALT BS Exercise 14

Whether your recovery involves sexual addiction or intimacy avoidance, this acronym represents daily feelings and pitfalls that can fluctuate your emotions and dive you into negative coping mechanisms. The more of these you have, the more likely you're to fall back into destructive behaviors or ways of thinking.

H.	Hungry	This involves not just how often you eat but how you eat
A.	Angry	Unchecked resentment or frustration can swell if not processed and shared
L.	Lonely	Avoiding interaction with your partner, family, and friends
T.	Tired	Quality, duration, and when you sleep or rest
B.	Bored	Time management, cultivating a rhythm of life, filling your time
S.	Stressed	How full is your plate? What do you do to de-stress?

(ALL Step Connection: We recover together)

There are a hundred different things you could do to keep your heart and body happy.

Make a plan for each area of health and share your plan with another in recovery.

Be willing to revise this plan as you go through recovery, so you can depend on what you need to maintain sobriety and health.

	Plan	Revisions
Hungry		
Angry		

1 Peter 1: 6-8 CEB You now rejoice in this hope, even if necessary for you to be distressed for a short time by various trials. This is necessary so that your faith may be found genuine. (Your faith is more valuable than gold, which will be destroyed even though it is itself tested by fire.} Your genuine faith will result in praise, glory, and honor for you when Jesus Christ is revealed. Although you've never seen him, you love him. Even though you don't see him now, you trust him and so rejoice with a glorious joy that is too much for words.

Father, HALT BS is not going to steal my reward. My faith is genuine. The distress caused by HALT BS is only for a short time. I can avoid HALT BS by making good choices. Thank You for Your grace so I can be successful. In Jesus' name, Amen.

Lonely		
Tired		
Bored		
Stressed		

PARTNER CONNECT Share your HALT BS plan with your partner.

RECOVERY TOOL BOX

Gratitude List Exercise 15

It is important to battle the cynical script, the negative things you think about your partner or others. This kind of thinking diminishes any positive thinking. Being thankful and being critical or judgmental cannot happen simultaneously. This is why this exercise is essential for your recovery and healing.

First, think about your partner. They are who you are most responsible for thinking positively about and expressing your gratitude towards. Next, the most important individuals to practice this with are your children and family. Then, consider any friends, coworkers, or others who may have hurt you that you will have to practice showing gratitude towards.

Brainstorm the people or groups that you can practice gratitude towards in the categories below.

Partner	
Kid/Family	
Friends	
Coworkers	
Others that have hurt you	

At the top of each column, fill in the 4 people/groups you will be writing gratitudes for during the next week. Then write 3 things you're grateful for about them for each day.

Day	_____	_____	_____	_____
1				
2				
3				
4				
5				

1 Thessalonians 5: 14b-18 AMP ...be very patient with everyone [always controlling your temper]. See that no one repays another with evil for evil, but always seek that which is good for one another and for all people. Rejoice always and delight in your faith; be unceasing and persistant in prayer; in every situation [no matter what the circumstances] be thankful and continually give thanks to God; for this is the will of God for you in Christ Jesus.

Father, according to Your word, You want me to be very patient with my partner, my children, extended family, my coworkers, and all people. I will take every thought captive and make it obedient to Your Word. I will purposely view the good in my partner and in all people, and pray for them continually, giving You thanks that they are in my life. It is Your will for me to do so. In Jesus' name, Amen

6				
7				

Step 8 Connection: In order to have an "attitude of gratitude" you will need to rely upon God to help you open your heart and change the way you see others. Write a prayer, inviting God to change the old ways of thinking that have led you to think critically and judge others.

PARTNER CONNECT Share at least one of the gratitudes you write about your partner daily with them.

Bookending

Exercise 16

Bookends hold things in place by standing before and after books on a shelf.

Similarly, this exercise is meant to create guardrails for entering any situation that challenges your recovery or sobriety. You make a call before and after the challenging event or situation.

Suppose you expect a situation in the coming week, hour, or day to be challenging. Can you think of a situation that will possibly tempt you sexually or challenge your intimacy with your partner? We know that in recovery it's not a matter of if, but when we will face challenges. We have a choice then: do we reach out, make a call, send a text, process the challenge with each other, pray for one another, and strengthen each other – or not? We are stronger together in community than we are isolated and alone.

At the end of the day, or rather at the beginning, you have a choice. So make the choice to use bookending for the next challenging situation you face.

Name 3 events or situations you WILL enter, where you would benefit from bookending:

Now, practice bookending. Like a journal entry, describe what you discussed, what you prayed with each other about, and how you benefited from using bookending.

Before	After
1.	1.
2.	2.
3.	3.

James 1:22-25 ERV Do what God's teaching says; don't just listen and do nothing. When you only sit and listen, you are fooling yourselves. Hearing God's teaching and doing nothing is like looking at your face in the mirror and doing nothing about what you saw. You go away and immediately forget how bad you looked. But when you look into God's perfect law that sets people free, pay attention to it. If you do what it says, you will have God's blessing. Never just listen to his teaching and forget what you heard.

Father, I understand that this teaching on bookending is for my own good and keeps me on the path of righteousness. I won't just listen to what my instructors tell me, but I will take these teachings to heart and act on them to the very best of my ability. Only then will You impart your blessings on me. I want my relationship with my partner blessed beyond measure and I position myself to receive Your blessing. In Jesus' name, Amen.

THE FOUNDATIONS OF RECOVERY - PART 1 GROUND ZERO

ALL Step Connection: "We" is a word used to emphasize a community of like-minded people seeking recovery. Explain why bookending could help you on your recovery journey.

PARTNER CONNECT Share what you learned about bookending and tell your partner who you are going to start bookending with. It is not necessary to share specific struggles that you need to bookend about.

12 Steps in a Year

Step 1   Exercise 17

We admitted we were powerless over our struggle and that our lives had become unmanageable

Goals

- Be honest with yourself.

This is going to feel like a radical shift from how you once lived inside. You are no longer alone, and your struggle is something that you must share with others in order to heal.

- You are not in control.

You want to begin the practice of letting go of thinking that you have control over how you act in your destructive coping strategies. You will discover certain daily practices of surrender, prayer, and boundaries that will help you in the fight against slipping back into destructive patterns

- Share the burden of recovery.

We join a recovery group with the hope that we can get help. That help first and foremost comes with making phone calls to others in recovery. The goal is 6/7 calls minimum per week. If needed, call more, whenever you are triggered into acting out. We will and can help each other find a better way to live.

Expectations

- This road of recovery requires routines, boundaries, and daily exercises to take action. Having vision or desire to recover is not enough. Action, or believed behavior, is what your loved ones will see as evidence of your recovery, because action makes your vision of healing become possible.
- Temptations will become less extreme the longer your sobriety lasts. Others in your recovery group will inspire you to press on, get back up, even after a slip. Listen to their guidance and put their feedback into action.

Hurdles

- Giving up control can feel counterintuitive.
  The 12 steps are built on the understanding that we cannot overcome our struggle with our own willpower, alone.

- You may reach desperation, a thirst, a drive inside you when you begin surrendering the areas of your life that you need help in. Pride will get in the way.

- Recovery is a marathon, not a sprint. Take everything one day at a time. Healing for yourself and loved ones will not happen in one day but is progressive.

- Remind yourself that you are worth it. You are worth healing, and you are worth the help others will give you through these desperate times.

Set a personal Goal, describe an Expectation you have, and state a Hurdle you can foresee or have.

Goal: Expectation: Hurdle:	**1 Peter 3:12 CEV The Lord watches over everyone who obeys him, and he listens to their prayers.** Father, I have decided to be integrous and ask for grace to do what is right in your sight. In Jesus' name, Amen.

PARTNER CONNECT Sometimes our loved ones can see things that we aren't aware of or have overlooked. Once you have set a personal goal and defined an expectation and a hurdle, share these with your partner. Ask for their input. Is there anything they're seeing that you aren't? If so, write it down.

Step 2

Exercise 18

We came to believe that a power greater than ourselves could restore us to sanity

Goals

- You begin exploring who or what God is and has been to you
- This is a searching and reflective time of recovery. In particular, your history with God is something you should reflect on.
- You will share this transformative time in Step 2 through daily routines of accepting your feelings, anxieties, and fears in prayer and fellowship throughout your day.
- Building off of Step 1, there is a desperation for healing that you must carry with you throughout recovery. Therefore, make the daily choice to believe healing is possible through God. This is a practice and action that you and you alone must choose.

Expectations

- Daily spiritual practices are essential to recovery.
- AM, PM, and daily surrendering prayers are foundational parts of recovery. Expect to be required to check in with how these practices are going.
- Share all your heart with God. Baring your thoughts, feelings, and temptations to Him is essential as you emerge from your old habits of hiding.

Hurdles

- Connecting to God can be mysterious and foreign.
- Start with recovery, surrender, and gratitude prayers to God.
- Seek others in recovery for advice and help with where to start. Remember it is one day at a time, one prayer at a time, and one choice at a time.
- Prayer can feel awkward and shameful following the weight of relationship destruction. Remember that God hears you and wants healing for you. God doesn't want the avoidant behaviors that brought you into recovery to be the end of your story. He wants you to live a life of health and have a victorious ending to your story.

What are your initial thoughts and feelings when you read "We came to believe that a power greater than ourselves could restore us to sanity?"

_____

_____

_____

_____

_____

_____

THE FOUNDATIONS OF RECOVERY - PART 1 GROUND ZERO

Set a personal Goal, describe an Expectation you have, and state a Hurdle you can foresee or have.

Goal:

Expectation:

Hurdle:

Hebrews 11:6 GNT No one can please God without faith, for whoever comes to God must have faith that God exists and rewards those who seek him.

Father, You are all powerful. Without You, I am nothing. But with You, I can do all things. In Jesus' name, Amen.

PARTNER CONNECT Share what you have learned about God with your partner and explain how this helps you.

Step 3   Exercise 19

We made a decision to turn our will and lives over to the care of God as we understand Him.

Goals

- This is a decision, not made in one day or in one minute, but every day, with every prayer, and with every phone-call cry for help as we live a different life from the one we lived before.
- We need to make and revise boundaries to keep us sober in our recovery whenever triggering situations arise.
- We live in fellowship, turning over our lives to God. This will involve honest assessment of the areas in our lives that may be unhealthy.

Expectations

- Freedom is found in full surrender.
- Our weaknesses are where we begin turning our lives over in order to receive healing and newfound strength.
- This is when we get into the details of where we need to turn over control. Whether finances or whatever way you withhold, you will need to examine anything and everything that you idolize and obsess over that takes the place of God in your heart.
- Sharing any anxiety or hesitation with those further in recovery will aid you in step 3.

Hurdles

- Turning over our lives could mean changing where we spend our time, money, and attention. The truths that God will begin revealing to you about unhealthy habits, relationships, and entertainment can be hard to accept.
- Trusting in God is easier said than done. This is a daily practice, and if done with honesty and submission, it will be a painful and rewarding battle won with God by your side.
- Moving on without fully submitting your life and will implies you aren't ready to move into Step 4. So slow down. One day at a time, seek God in prayer and turn to others for help. Remember, you are worth it!

Set a personal Goal, describe an Expectation you have, and state a Hurdle you can foresee or have.

Goal:

Expectation:

Hurdle:

1 John 5:14, 15 ESV And this is the confidence that we have toward him, that if we ask anything according to his will he hears us. And if we know that he hears us in whatever we ask, we know that we have the requests that we have asked of him.

Father, thank You for keeping me strong in all of these steps throughout each and every day. In Jesus' name, Amen.

PARTNER CONNECT Make a list of at least 3 things you need to turn over to God. Ask your partner for help making this list. Also, share with your partner your goal date to complete this step and who you have designated as an accountability partner. If it is someone from group, be sure to share only the first name to honor confidentiality.

Step 4   Exercise 20

We made a searching and fearless moral inventory of ourselves.

Goals

- This is where honesty gets put into action. Document and reflect on your past regarding:
  - Harms done to me
  - Harms done to others
  - My tendencies toward others
- We reflect upon how we acted out or withheld, why we acted out or withheld, and the feelings that we associate with the actions that we committed or that were done to us.

Expectations

- By listing out our history, we begin searching for full honesty with God and others.
- We may need to add to our inventory as time passes.
- It is not necessary to disclose your inventory. Talking to a recovery coach, a therapist, or a trusted spiritual leader will create a safe space to vent feelings associated with revisiting the past.
- Disclosure in a marriage may be necessary BUT be sure to create plans for such a disclosure with appropriate planning and guidance. Use individual and couples' recovery counseling or coaching.
- Becoming Well providers are an option for help with this process. We can create a safe space for such a disclosure to happen with the least amount of pain possible.
- We have experience and are certified and trained, but we also know firsthand from our own history of recovery that disclosure can look many different ways for different couples. The key is to be honest to the extent that it will help your partner feel safe.

Hurdles

- Emotions are raw when listing your history of destruction. At this point, leaning on God and recovery partners will be essential to overcome the inevitable grief you will feel while recording your inventory.
  - Have a list of people to call handy whenever you're working through your inventory.
- You may feel broken and not worthy of healing while listing out the pain you have caused others.
  - Return to the foundation of Steps 1, 2, and 3, and remind yourself that God wants nothing less than to free you from your broken ways of thinking.
- Adjust your daily recovery prayers to grieve the pain and seek God for the strength to live a life in full surrender.
- Seek others in recovery who have experienced the freedom from completing an exhaustive Step 4 inventory. This step can and should be thorough. Take your time, because it will be worth the effort.

Set a personal Goal, describe an Expectation you have, and state a Hurdle you can foresee or have.

Goal:

Expectation:

Hurdle:

PARTNER CONNECT After you take your "fearless moral inventory," be sure to get input from your partner. Ask them to name 3 things they see in your character that you should work on. Does their list coincide with yours? Do they have input that is different from the things you thought of? Are they right? If so, write down what they told you.

Ecclesiastes 9:17, 18 CEV Words of wisdom spoken softly make much more sense than the shouts of a ruler to a crowd of fools. Wisdom is more powerful than weapons, yet one mistake can destroy all the good you have done.

Father, give me grace to be brutally honest with myself as I write down the issues that I deal with on a daily basis. I will not minimize or rationalize my conduct but face them with the attitude that I am an overcomer! In Jesus' name, Amen.

Step 5   Exercise 21

We admitted to God, to ourselves, and to others the exact nature of our wrongs.

Goals

- This is where you become fully vulnerable – an open book – about your history, to God and to others.
  - You will share your inventory with a recovery partner.
  - Disclosure to your significant other may be overdue and needed, so you will need to seek help in how to give a full disclosure. Becoming Well can help with that. So can any other trained recovery coach or counselor who specializes in disclosures.
- Admitting to God is an ongoing process. Accepting the nature of your wrongs is an intimate process that starts with daily honesty with God.
- Aim to fit time into your daily prayers and recovery work to speak light to your inventory, sharing it with God.

Expectations

- Sharing your story will be freeing and uplifting. You will see a huge stride in momentum in your recovery during this step.
  - Keeping this momentum is important to be able to complete the 12-step process.
- The peace you feel from being open and honest, for maybe the first time ever, can be an exciting rush.
  - Therefore, that freedom is very personal. Others may not be feeling the freedom you are. They may expect you to remain under the pain they're still experiencing.
- Whatever it is that you may have said to yourself, "I will take this to my grave" is exactly what you need to share with another and confess to God. Your healing and recovery depend on it.

Hurdles

- Fear and secrecy can get in the way of being vulnerable and honest. The lies that your pain and addiction or avoidance will tell you can get in the way of your recovery and healing.
- As mentioned before, loved ones may negatively view your freedom and relief in being completely honest, especially anyone you have betrayed.
  - Be prepared to use tools to give space for their feelings of pain that persist or flare up. It is understandable for them to still feel pain.

If you need help understanding the other person's feelings, consult with a Becoming Well provider or other trained professionals.

- Always, always remember: you are worth recovery.

Set a personal Goal, describe an Expectation you have, and state a Hurdle you can foresee or have.

Goal:

Expectation:

Hurdle:

PARTNER CONNECT What was the biggest thing you learned from this step? Share that learning with your partner.

Proverbs 28:13 CEV If you don't confess your sins, you will be a failure. But God will be merciful if you confess your sins and give them up.

Father, give me the grace to be brutally honest with myself. As I communicate my harmful actions, I will be accurate in judgement and wise in finding the words to express my concerns in a manner to reduce the harmful impact to my wounded partner. In Jesus' name, Amen.

Step 6   Exercise 22

We were entirely ready to have God remove all these defects of character.

Goals

- Here's where we become ready for change.
    - It may include giving up habits, attitudes, or ways of thinking.
    - Whatever the defect is that you identified in your inventory, your target in this step is to prepare your heart for putting those behaviors behind you.
- Be open to feedback and reflection.
    - If your actions are still a reflection of your defects, then you will need to be open to humility.
    - In this process, you may need to add to and record an ongoing inventory.

Expectations

- This step will consolidate and summarize the defects you identified in your inventory.
- You will need to share this process of summing up your flaws with others in recovery.
- Healing involves simply saying out loud that you are ready. Pray regularly, AM, PM, and throughout the day to prepare for God to help you remove your character defects.

Hurdles

- Being ready for defects to be removed may involve removing unhealthy habits, pastimes, or relationships from your life.
    - Help from others in recovery and God will reveal aspects of your life that need to be removed.
    - Removing your defects can be painful, like going into surgery. Exercises like appreciation and resignation letters can help with letting things go from your past.
- Seek guidance from others in recovery and hear how they became ready for God to remove their character defects.
- Keeping true to daily submission, this is a one-day-at-a-time process. Let go and allow God and others to help you prepare to move past your character defects and into a new life.

What are your initial thoughts and feelings when you read "We were entirely ready to have God remove all these defects of character?"

_____

_____

_____

_____

_____

_____

Set a personal Goal, describe an Expectation you have, and state a Hurdle you can foresee or have.

Goal:

Expectation:

Hurdle:

PARTNER CONNECT With your partner, share any hurdle you identified in completing this step. Tell them who you are going to be accountable to in order to overcome this hurdle.

Ephesians 4:22-24 CEV You were told that your foolish desires will destroy you and that you must give up your old way of life with all its bad habits. Let the Spirit change your way of thinking and make you into a new person. You were created to be like God, and so you must please him and be truly holy.

Father, I give You my mind and my heart. I choose to throw away my former lifestyle and bad habits. I allow the Spirit of the Living God to help me to renew my mind so I can have the thoughts, feelings, and purposes of Your heart. In Jesus' name, Amen.

Step 7 Exercise 23

We humbly asked God to remove our shortcomings.

Goals

- This is a process of practicing full surrender.
    - Create prayers to God, asking Him to remove your character defects.
    - Imagine what life would be like without your struggle
- Ongoing Inventory needs to be taken daily
    - When a defect arises, return to asking God for its removal

Expectations

- Full recovery involves sharing your struggles with others. This is a key way to involve others and God in the process of removal.
- Some keys to success are:
    - Trusting fully in God.
    - Believing that God can help.
- Strong emotion may rush out when you're imagining the removal of your defect.
- The feeling of desperation is good.
- Thirsting for a new way of living, provided by God, is a gift.

Hurdles

- **This is the place where you've passed the halfway mark through the 12 steps, so don't give up!**
- Half efforts now will yield half results later.
- Practicing forgiving yourself, one defect at a time, and asking for their removal one at a time is how you begin to love yourself and, in turn, become able to love others fully.

What are your initial thoughts and feelings when you read "We humbly asked God to remove our shortcomings?"

_____
_____
_____
_____
_____
_____
_____

Set a personal Goal, describe an Expectation you have, and state a Hurdle you can foresee or have.

Goal:

Expectation:

Hurdle:

PARTNER CONNECT Identify at least one area where you think you're giving a "half effort" or less than a full effort. Share this with your partner and tell them who you are going to be accountable to in order to overcome this challenge.

James 4:7, 8 & 10 CEV Surrender to God! Resist the devil, and he will run from you. Come near to God, and he will come near to you. Clean up your lives, you sinners. Purify your hearts, you people who can't make up your mind...Be humble in the Lord's presence, and he will honor you.

Father, I humbly surrender to Your word, Your ways, and Your purposes. Only humility and obedience to You will give me the authority to drive the devil out of my life. I take my shield of faith and quench every fiery dart. Greater is He who lives in me than he who is wordly! In Jesus' name, Amen.

Step 8 — Exercise 24

We made a list of all people we had harmed, and we became willing to make amends to them all

Goals

- Reflect on all the people and organizations you wronged from your inventory.
- If you think of someone or some group you have missed, list them out as well in this step.
- Become clear on what making amends is and what it isn't.
- Have multiple discussions with those who have completed amends before. Take notes on how it went for them.

Become willing by God's strength, not your own. Surrender personal judgements and seek to forgive prior to entering an amends.

Expectations

- Amends Is NOT...
    - Expecting forgiveness from the person you harmed.
    - About sharing reasons for your struggles.
    - Placing blame for your struggles on traumas you've endured.
    - Expecting the other party to own their wrongs.
- Amends Is...
    - Communicating your faults and taking responsibility.
    - Recognizing the pain you have caused.
    - Asking for forgiveness.
- Becoming willing is another process involving prayer.
- Forgiving others for their wrongs frees you to be able to love them from this day on, whether they want to reconcile a relationship with you or not.

Hurdles

- Feelings can get in the way of making your amends
    - These include anger, resentment, pride, malice... basically anything that breeds a defensive or entitled stance.
    - Unforgiveness is at the root of your judgment towards someone. Forgiving them says, "I am handing their judgment over to God."
- Becoming willing to make amends can look different depending on if a face-to-face amends will harm someone. Being willing to give a face-to-face amends is best, but Step 9 will explore other options.
- Owning up to your role in causing others pain can be frightening. Asking God for the courage you need can be added to your daily prayers. Discuss such hesitancies with someone in recovery. Remember, you are worth it to God and your loved ones to own your mistakes.

Set a personal Goal, describe an Expectation you have, and state a Hurdle you can foresee or have.

Goal:

Expectation:

Hurdle:

PARTNER CONNECT Your partner should be on your list for amends. Ask them to write you a letter explaining ways in which you have hurt them. Understanding specifics will help you as you prepare to make amends. You may not agree with everything in their letter. If you are struggling to see things from their point of view, ask one of your fellow group members, a coach, or a trusted friend to help you see things from their perspective.

Matthew 5: 23, 24 MSG This is how I want you to conduct yourself in these matters. If you enter your place of worship and, about to make an offering, you suddenly remember a grudge a friend has against you, abandon your offering, leave immediately, go to this friend and make things right. Then and only then, come back and work things out with God.

Father, You want me to be in the right relationship with my fellow man. You even expect me to be accountable with my peers before I can even give You an offering! That's how important it is to You that I make amends with all people. I will be honorable and make amends immediately according to Your word. In Jesus' name, Amen.

Step 9

Exercise 25

We made direct amends to such people wherever possible, except when to do so would injure them or others.

Goals

- Decide who you can deliver an amends face-to-face to.
  - This will be a hard decision and will depend on whether giving a face-to-face amends will harm the person you have wronged, and whether or not they will want to receive your amends.
  - Counsel from others who have given their amends before is essential.
- Write amends to every person or group from your inventory whom you have harmed. This is a healing process for you.

You will need to read your rough drafts to someone experienced in giving amends and make revisions.

- And finally, give your amends.

Expectations

- So here it is, RUT-ABC
  - R - Recognize the Wrong
  - U - Understanding the Hurt
  - T - Take Responsibility
  - A - Ask for Forgiveness
  - BC - Behavior Change

> **1 Peter 5:5 TLB** You younger men, follow the leadership of those who are older. And all of you serve each other with humble spirits, for God gives special blessings to those who are humble, but sets himself against those who are proud.
>
> Father, I humble myself before You and before those whom I have harmed. I choose to use wisdom and make amends to the best of my ability. I take responsibility for my actions and ask for forgiveness. My behavior will be godly from this day forward. In Jesus' name, Amen.

- You will use your inventory to direct much of this process. There is a lot of explanation for what Amends is, what it isn't, and what each part of RUT-ABC should look like.
- This process can take a substantial amount of time. It is understandable. Practice delivering the amends that are more challenging and prepare for the possible feelings the receiver may have.

Hurdles

- Their feelings may be centered on pain and anger.
  - Expect to stand under their feelings.
  - You will need to prepare for how they may react to you asking for forgiveness. If emotions are high, you may need to prepare some diffusing strategies. Seek counsel on such strategies from others more experienced at giving amends.
- God will be your strength through the amends-writing process and when you're giving the amends.
  - Your dependence upon God will be tested.
  - You are worth owning your defects and how they have caused pain to others. Remember that giving your amends and moving towards reconciliation is going to strengthen your recovery and your relationship with God.

THE FOUNDATIONS OF RECOVERY - PART 1 GROUND ZERO

Set a personal Goal, describe an Expectation you have, and state a Hurdle you can foresee or have.

Goal:

Expectation:

Hurdle:

PARTNER CONNECT It is crucial that you don't ask your partner to accept any responsibility for the things you have done. Make sure you have worked through any resentments you hold against your partner before making amends to them. Avoid making your amends about you in any way, including putting pressure on your partner to forgive you and/or "get over it." Check your needs at the door so that your amends can be as heartfelt as possible.

Step 10   Exercise 26

We continue to take personal inventory and when we were wrong, promptly admitted it

Goals

- From this point on, the end of this process is only the beginning.
  - The purpose of the 12 steps is to give you a new way to live your life. The primary way we do this in recovery is to have an open, honest, and ongoing personal inventory.
- Honesty is the goal, the main goal, the only goal in this step.

Expectations

- Your routines will begin to change.
  - Daily recovery work will begin evolving into fewer questions to answer in the step work and more reflection about everyday living.
- Immediately admitting you're wrong should be something you are practicing regularly already with weekly check-ins.
- Honesty has become a way of living now, and going back to secrecy needs to be a thing of the past.

Hurdles

- Temptation will always be present in your life of recovery.
  - The truth is that we all slip and are not perfect.
  - Secrecy will be a temptation that can set you back, returning to steps 1, 2, and 3.
- Remember the cost and destruction from your behaviors.
- This step is the launching point into lifelong healing and recovery. Even when the 12 steps are over, the fight isn't.
- You are worth a life of authentic relationships and freedom from your withholding behaviors.

What are your initial thoughts and feelings when you read "We continue to take personal inventory and, when we were, promptly admitted it"?

_____
_____
_____
_____
_____
_____
_____

Set a personal Goal, describe an Expectation you have, and state a Hurdle you can foresee or have.

Goal:

Expectation:

Hurdle:

PARTNER CONNECT It is crucial for the health of your recovery that you take your inventory at the end of each day to identify any ways in which you have been wrong and/or hurt others. This week, ask your partner if there is anything you have said and done that they need you to apologize for.

Proverbs 11:3 CEV If you do the right thing, honesty will be your guide. But if you are crooked, you will be trapped by your own dishonesty.

Father, give me the grace to live a transparent life and to be honest in every aspect. I choose to wear truth and faithfulness like a garland around my neck. I want to be known as a person of integrity. In Jesus' name, Amen.

Step 11   Exercise 27

We seek to improve contact with God through prayer and meditation, praying for knowledge of God's will for our lives and the power to carry it out.

Goals

- We started with relying upon God, and we end with relying upon God
- Creating ongoing habits, devotionals, and meditations will center your life on a will greater than your own
- Continue to build upon your current relationship with God

Claim a life of peace with God as your provider, not people, not materials, not your past coping mechanisms.

Expectations

- Your spiritual walk is only as good as how much effort you put into it.
  - This is your daily choice to put God or idols first in your heart.
- Surrendering your own will and seeking God's will for your life is a practice, not a faucet or light switch.
- Whether in good times or desperate ones, you will continue to need to seek God in order to seek ongoing recovery.

Hurdles

- Feelings are not always something to be followed:
  - Our own will gets in the way sometimes
  - Thinking you've got it under control will lead to arrogance and pride
  - Boasting will lead to self-centeredness
- Remember how God has helped you in this walk of recovery. He will be what leads you into a life of walking in humility and peace.

What are your initial thoughts and feelings when you read "We seek to improve contact with God through prayer and meditation, praying for knowledge of God's will for our lives and the power to carry it out?"

_____
_____
_____
_____
_____
_____

Set a personal Goal, describe an Expectation you have, and state a Hurdle you can foresee or have.

Goal:

Expectation:

Hurdle:

PARTNER CONNECT If prayer is a part of your daily life, ask your partner to join in prayer with you each day. If not, share with your partner what you have been learning about daily interactions with God.

Isaiah 41:13 KJV **For I the Lord thy God will hold thy right hand, saying unto thee, Fear not; I will help thee.**

Father, I choose to make my relationship with You the first priority in my life because I know without You, I am dust. I choose to begin my morning with You. I choose to be in Your presence all day long as I go about my tasks, and I choose to be in Your presence when I lay down at night. I'm aware that You live in me and know my every thought, word, and deed before they even happen. This keeps me in the straight and narrow. I love You and choose to serve You all the days of my life. In Jesus' name, Amen.

Step 12 — Exercise 28

Having had a spiritual awakening from our experience through the steps, we seek to share with others and practice our principles in all our relationships

Goals

- Pray for God to use you, and to open doors to what may come next in your walk of recovery.
- Assess the season you're in.
- Stay connected with others in recovery even after commencing.
- Commencement means you aren't finished yet and will always be in the process.

Expectations

- You can develop purpose for your life in recovery.
    - God can use you and your story to impact the lives of others if you allow it.
    - Relationships with those seeking a better, freer life from struggles will be more vulnerable and loving
- Behaviors that you keep and take with you will be the evidence of real change.

Hurdles

- Closing yourself off to God or His purposes can feel tempting.
    - Keeping your story to yourself
    - Thinking you've got this now on your own
    - Resorting to old habits out of resentment from lost relationships
- Remember that God wants a new life for you. You are worth lifelong healing and recovery.
- With the progress you've made, practice gratitude, and use any exercise up until this point whenever you need.
- Keep going, keep relying, keep believing that you are worth it!

What are your initial thoughts and feelings when you read "Having had a spiritual awakening from our experience through the steps, we seek to share with others and practice our principles in all our relationships?"

_____
_____
_____
_____
_____
_____
_____

Set a personal Goal, describe an Expectation you have, and state a Hurdle you can foresee or have.

Goal:

Expectation:

Hurdle:

<u>PARTNER CONNECT</u> Share with your partner the name of at least one person you plan to share your story with.

> 2 Timothy 1: 8, 9 CEB Don't be ashamed of the testimony about the Lord or of me, his prisoner. Instead, share the suffering for the good news, depending on God's power. God is the one who saved and called us with a holy calling. This wasn't based on what we have done, but it was based on his own purpose and grace that he gave us in Christ Jesus before time began.
>
> Father, open doors for me and use me for Your glory. Anoint me to help others leave this oppressed lifestyle so they may live the abundant life! Thank You for all You have done for me. Thank You for bringing opportunities to improve the quality of their lives because of Jesus' sacrifice. In Jesus' name, Amen.

Helping My Partner Heal
(Part 1)

HELPING MY PARTNER HEAL (PART 1)

Rebuilding Trust Pyramid – Honesty

Exercise 29

The first layer of the rebuilding trust pyramid is honesty. Honesty is the foundation of trust in all healthy relationships. Without honesty, relationships fail to thrive. When we work with wounded partners, they often tell us that the lies they were told by the wounding partner are just as hard, if not harder, to move past than the betrayal-related behavior. Lying, for most wounded partners, represents multiple betrayals. These betrayals often make them feel disrespected and foolish. Not only did the wounding partner break the agreement between the couple when they engaged in the betrayal-related behavior, but they lied about it. This causes the wounded partner to call into question everything that happened before and after the lies were told.

If honesty cannot be established, what remains is a relationship devoid of trust and intimacy.

If a couple is to have a chance at rebuilding their relationship after betrayal, it must be built on a foundation of honesty and transparency. Ongoing lying and dishonesty will send the wounded partner the message that the wounding partner is primarily concerned with their own comfort, even if it is at the expense of the wounded partner's heart.

Step 1 Connection:

ba. In your own words, why is honesty the foundation of your relationship(s)?

bb. Name three topics you recall in the past where your lying was automatic, a powerlessness to protect yourself.

1.	2.	3.

> **Ephesians 4:15 MSG God wants us to grow up, to tell the whole truth in love - like Christ did in everything.**
>
> Father, You want me to be a mature Christian and in order to be mature, I must tell the entire truth with all sincerity. Give me the grace to be perfectly honest and protect the heart of my wounded partner. In Jesus' name, Amen.

PARTNER CONNECT Honesty is not only foundational to a trusting relationship with your partner; it is foundational to your personal recovery as well. Honesty fosters intimacy, but it also helps with self-awareness. It holds us accountable to ourselves, too. When we are dishonest with others, we are first dishonest with ourselves. When we break trust with others by being dishonest, we break trust with ourselves. Shame is a major reason we are dishonest. Something you can do with your partner to help you reduce shame is the "Worst Moment of the Day" exercise. If your partner is willing, add this exercise to your dailies. It's simple: tell your partner one moment of the day that was your worst moment. A moment when you weren't proud of how you behaved or what you thought. (Be careful that you don't tell your partner something bad you thought about them, as this will hurt them and cause discord.) If they are willing, they will listen to what you said and say, "Thank you for telling me. I love you anyway."

HELPING MY PARTNER HEAL (PART 1)

Rebuilding Trust Pyramid – Exercise 30 Safety

When we speak with wounded partners who have been hurt by their partner's betrayal-related behavior, they almost always describe feeling unsafe. First and foremost, this is because the predictability of the relationship is now gone. This typically initiates a fight-or-flight response from the wounded partner because the wounding partner's actions have caused betrayal trauma. Unfortunately, it can take the wounded partner weeks and months (in some cases longer) before their body and mind stop reacting to the trauma. Safety in the relationship must be re-established if the wounded partner is ever to get out of a hypervigilant mode of operation. In the case of relationships where intimacy avoidance is present, safety may never have been properly established in the first place.

When betrayal occurs, it can cause a lack of safety in several areas. The **types of safety** that are most often violated are physical/sexual, emotional, and commitment. Fill out the blank below to determine and understand the type of safety your wife/partner is requesting:

"My wife says she needs _____ to feel safe."

Some more examples: She needs: your attention, you to stop lying, to communicate with her better or more, to be more vulnerable, to be heard, you to be consistent, to install a tracking app on your phone, respect, to stop sexually pressuring her, transparency, honesty, to look at your phone, reassurance, emotional support, to share your struggles.

In the table below, name the "area" where you have created a lack of safety (use the **types of safety** listed above) and name an action to begin creating safety. Call others who are further along in recovery about their experiences and ideas for creating safety. Discuss your ideas with your partner as well.

Types of Safety	Plan of Action

Proverbs 19:22,23 TLB Kindness makes a man attractive. And it is better to be poor than dishonest. Reverence for God gives life, happiness and protection from harm.

Father, grace me with kindness and honesty so my wounded partner can heal from my transgression. Strengthen me so I can be honorable and protect myself and my wounded partner from harm. Thank you for empowering me to understand my role in this relationship and the heavy responsibility to keep us safe and secure in each other. In Jesus' name, Amen.

THE FOUNDATIONS OF RECOVERY - PART 1 GROUND ZERO

PARTNER CONNECT Once you have completed the exercise, share it with your partner. Ask them if they have further input. If they do, add what they say to your exercise.

Rebuilding Trust Pyramid – Exercise 31 Consistency

The third layer of the rebuilding trust pyramid is consistency.

Consistency is an important ingredient in trust because it shows the wounded partner that they can depend on the wounding partner to follow through. When we work with couples to develop plans to create safety, we always explain that, without consistency, those plans are basically useless. When the wounding partner engages in infidelity-related behavior, they send a message to the wounded partner that they can't be trusted to uphold the promises and agreements that are important to the health of the relationship. If the wounding partner wants their partner to accept that they can change this, they must be consistent.

What is going to show Consistency To your partner?

Here's a place to start:

1. Refer to any exercise you have done so far in The Becoming Well Workgroup program
2. Refer to the past two exercises on safety and honesty
3. Refer to others in recovery, asking them what evidence of consistency there has been in their relationship
4. Create consequences for yourself (e.g., No electronic devices for a week, 25 push-ups, eat an onion...)

Consistency Behavior	Day(s) of the Week	My Consequence if I Don't Follow Through or Reward if you do
	M T W Th F Sa Su	
	M T W Th F Sa Su	
	M T W Th F Sa Su	

**1 Corinthians 15:58 MSG
With all this going for us, my dear, dear friends, stand your ground. And don't hold back. Throw yourselves into the work of the Master, confident that nothing you do for him is a waste of time or effort.**

Father, the time, effort and energy I formerly practiced in doing evil, I will now use for good. Every micro and macro decision will be consistently godly and pleasing to You and to my wounded partner. I will throw myself into healing my relationship with my wounded partner. I ask You to make this relationship ALL that You created it to be. In Jesus' name, Amen.

	M T W Th F Sa Su	
	M T W Th F Sa Su	
	M T W Th F Sa Su	
	M T W Th F Sa Su	

PARTNER CONNECT Designate at least one person to whom you are going to be accountable for your plan. Share this exercise with your partner for extra accountability.

Rebuilding Trust Pyramid – Intimacy

Exercise 32

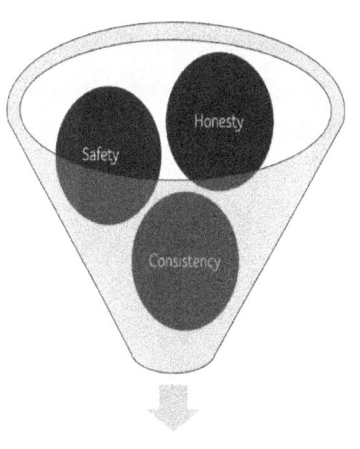

INTIMACY

The fourth and final layer of the rebuilding trust pyramid is intimacy. When we think of intimacy, people tend to jump straight to sex. Although this is one type of intimacy and is often an expression of other types, it is not the only one.

Some common areas of intimacy that a couple can share are created by:

- sharing emotions
- resolving conflict successfully
- sharing goals and dreams
- sharing and respecting each other's thoughts and opinions
- connecting around religion and spiritual ideas and beliefs, and
- sharing hobbies and interests.

The feelings of devastation, betrayal, loneliness, ambivalence, and confusion caused by betrayal cause a breakdown in intimacy between partners. One of the reasons for this is that these feelings can cause one or both parties in the relationship to withdraw. Although this is common for a period when infidelity is discovered or disclosed, both partners will need to recommit to the relationship if trust is to be restored.

In the case of relationships where intimacy avoidance is present, little to no intimacy was present in the relationship prior to the discovery or disclosure of betrayal.

When we test couples for the strength of their relationship structures, we typically find that most of these are completely missing. The issues caused by intimacy avoidance and self-centered behavior leave the relationship weak. Adding betrayal to this already weak structure makes it extremely difficult for couples dealing with these issues to survive, unless the intimacy avoidant is willing to admit the totality of their bad behavior and begin recovery right away.

Intimacy will be built all along the recovery journey, and the "ingredients" of honesty, safety, and consistency are what produce intimacy.

Sign and date here to make a commitment to God, your partner, your family, and yourself, that you will work to consistently create safety and trust in your relationship.

I, _____(name),

commit on _____(date).

Signature_____

Song of Solomon 2:13b, 14b Rise up, my love, my beautiful one, and come away...let me see your face, let me hear your voice; for your voice is sweet, and your face is lovely.

Father, give me grace to share my emotions, goals, and dreams with my beloved. I will also share my thoughts, opinions, hobbies, interests, and spiritual beliefs with them. Help us to be vulnerable and to successfully achieve the life goals that You established for us as a couple. In Jesus' name, Amen.

PARTNER CONNECT Ask your partner what types of intimacy they feel are most lacking in your relationship. Make a plan with your partner to address their top 2 intimacy concerns.

Standing Shoulder to Shoulder   Exercise 33

Why is it important for us to stand shoulder to shoulder with our partner in their pain?

As the wounding partner, one straightforward reason is that we've created quite a bit of pain for the wounded partner.

Our partner is in pain for lots of different reasons. In the beginning of the couple's recovery process, we're mostly standing shoulder to shoulder and helping them to heal from the pain that we've created. As we help our partners heal from much of the pain we've created, they start sharing other areas of their life that they've experienced or are currently experiencing pain.

So how do we stand shoulder to shoulder with our partner in their pain?

We use the empathy exercise.

We use speaker-listener strategies to make sure that they know that we're hearing them.

We set aside time on a weekly basis to have them share their pain with us so that we can help them process it

We decided that we're going to be a healing agent, not a re-wounding agent as they share pain with us.

We investigate and hear what they're saying rather than defending or refuting what they're saying.

All these are tools in this exercise book. We lean into the storm rather than run away from the storm.

Review the exercises in this book or other programs you've entered to help your partner heal and complete an "I will…" sentence for each.

I will…
I will…
I will…
I will…

I will…
I will…
I will…
I will…
Use more paper if needed

Early in recovery, as well as throughout recovery, we stand shoulder to shoulder with our partners. This means choosing to stand with our partners as they're going through the pain rather than creating more pain for them or abandoning them in their pain.

What days each week can you set aside to go to your partner and say, "is there anything that's happened to create pain for you for you?"

When our partner does bring their anger, complaints, or sadness to us, the key is to be purposeful and intentional.

To stand shoulder to shoulder, you need to not defend, explain, or correct them.

To stand shoulder to shoulder, you must learn to put yourself in their shoes (empathy).

Standing shoulder to shoulder with them does not mean that you agree with what they're saying, or that what they're saying is completely accurate, as that's not relevant. What is relevant is that they're experiencing pain, and you must show you care about them and want to help.

HELPING MY PARTNER HEAL (PART 1)

What pain statements have they made recently? How about in the past year? How can you stand with them shoulder to shoulder?

Step 8 Connection: Write a prayer to open your heart to hear your partner's pain and bear it with them, and the patience to hear it without defending, explaining, or offering advice. Write this prayer on a flash card. As you get home from work or return to your partner, you can prepare your demeanor to engage with your partner in love and kindness.

Ecclesiastes 4:10 CEB If either should fall, one can pick up the other. But how miserable are those who fall and don't have a companion to help them up!

Father, give me the grace to stand shoulder to shoulder with my partner and lift them up when they do fall down. I do not want my partner to be alone, abandoned and experiencing more pain in their lives. Cause me to be understanding, supportive, a good listener, and a helpmate. It is my responsibility to help my partner heal completely and as quickly as possible. If I do my part, Lord, You will do the rest. In Jesus' name, Amen.

PARTNER CONNECT Share your answers to steps one and two of this exercise with your partner.

Demeanor - Part 1   Exercise 34

Until the wounded partner feels a great deal of safety within the relationship, little-to-no progress will be made toward rebuilding trust. One of the main ways that safety can begin to be reestablished — or established for the first time, in the case of an intimacy avoidant relationship — is through the demeanor of the wounding partner.

If the wounding partner continues to be resistant to recovery or acts prideful, defensive, and/or arrogant, the wounded partner will not feel safe enough to engage in the recovery of the relationship. It is not enough to end the betrayal-related behavior, although this is extremely important.

The wounding partner also needs to be able to show true remorse for their actions. Arrogance, pride, and defensiveness send the wounded partner the message that the wounding partner is not truly sorry for what they have done and/or does not understand the effect that their actions have had on their partner.

When a wounding partner engages in infidelity-related behavior, they selfishly set the wounded partner aside in favor of something else. As a result, the wounded partner feels disrespected, unimportant, and forgotten. This is why it is of the utmost importance that the wounding partner show that they will do whatever it takes to win their partner back.

If the wounding partner continues to display a lack of humility by acting defensive, arrogant, or prideful, they inadvertently convey the message to the wounded partner that they should not ask for what they need in order to heal. Instead, they should just be happy with whatever the wounding partner is willing to give.

A defensive, prideful, or arrogant demeanor on the wounding partner's part sends the message that they do not value their partner. Someone with this type of demeanor needs to ask themselves why anyone would want to stay with someone who shows them this type of disrespect.

Why should anyone stay with a person who could cast them aside in an act of unfaithfulness and then continue to act remorseless about it and/or protect their own self-interest? When we view things in this light, we begin to understand how gracious the wounded partner is being by offering the wounding partner another chance.

What does it look like to show remorse?

[ ]

Exercise: Look in the mirror. Display remorse with your posture, body language, and facial expression. Hold this position and picture the feelings your partner has.

What feelings do you have about the devastation you've caused?

[ ]

Step Connection: What actions do you do on a day-to-day basis to show your partner an understanding, caring, and empathic demeanor?

> **Ephesians 4:2,3 CEB Conduct yourselves with all humility, gentleness and patience. Accept each other with love, and make an effort to preserve the unity of the Spirit with the peace that ties you together.**
>
> Father, grace me with the diligence to consistently practice patience and love towards my wounded partner, so that they may heal and we can bond in complete unity once more. In Jesus' name, Amen.

PARTNER CONNECT With your partner, take the 5 Apology Languages Quiz at https://5lovelanguages.com/quizzes/apology-language. Have a discussion with your partner regarding what makes an apology meaningful to them. Take notes and put what they told you, along with your own answers, in the box designated "What does it look like to show remorse?"

70/30 to 80/20

Exercise 35

In our work, we've found that when couples come to us, the wounding partner – the person who's bringing the sexual betrayal, the intimacy-avoidant behavior, etc. – is usually bringing 70% to 80% of the problems in the relationship.

Does the other partner bring problems and pain to the relationship? Absolutely. However, all pain is not created equal. In using relationship-ending behaviors and ways of thinking, the wounding partner's percentage to take responsibility for is much greater.

Here's the good news if you're in a relationship like this, where you are responsible for most of the relationship problems. You can heal 70 to 80% of the struggles in the relationship. That means that you can bring the relationship to a B or a C grade just by doing your part.

Think of it as first, second, third, and fourth gears. You need to keep it in first gear, which is working on yourself, and second gear, which is making things safe for your partner. This is a part of your 70 to 80% recovery work.

Reflect on your recovery so far. What actions are you taking that are evidence of you taking responsibility?

[ ]

What behaviors do you need to improve in or begin in order to reach a B or a C for the relationship?

[ ]

Step 5 Connection: On a recovery call this week, confess the areas you need to be held accountable for. Ask them how they are doing. Make this kind of accountability on a phone call a normal part of your weekly calls.

<u>PARTNER CONNECT</u> At a time when things are calm, ask your partner what you could do better to take accountability for ways you have hurt the relationship. Make sure you are prepared to hear what they have to say without defending yourself or getting angry. You can do this by making a recovery phone call ahead of time. After you have listened to your partner's point of view and validated their experience, make a recovery phone call to help yourself process what they have said to you.

> **1 Thessalonians 5:20-24 MSG** On the other hand, don't be gullible. Check out everything, and keep only what's good. Throw out anything tainted with evil. May God himself, the God who makes everything holy and whole, make you holy and whole, put you together-spirit, soul, and body-and keep you fit for the coming of our Master, Jesus Christ. The One who called you is completely dependable. If he said it, he'll do it!

> Father, research shows that intimacy avoidant behavior brings 70-80% of the problems into my relationship. I will follow Jesus' example. He was transparent and loving to all of His sheep. My spouse is a gift to me, and You have deposited my spouse under my care. I will be a good steward of this relationship and correct any intimacy avoidant behaviors in my character. I have the mind of Christ and hold the thoughts, feelings, and purposes of His heart concerning every situation. In Jesus' name, Amen.

Exercise 36 — **Stabilization**

We use the term "stabilization" to describe a phenomenon common to intimacy-avoidant relationships.

Let's pretend that your relationship is on a scale. On this scale, positive 4 represents the closest you can be with your partner emotionally, while -4 represents the furthest away you can be emotionally from your partner. Intimacy avoidants are uncomfortable with emotional closeness. As a result, they tend to keep the relationship at about a -1. The partner is unhappy enough to keep their distance, but not so dissatisfied that they want to leave.

Over time, IA behavior begins to "move the needle" on relationship satisfaction. The other partner starts to become more and more disgruntled. Their unhappiness moves them to a -2, then a -3, and so on. They soon become so unhappy that they start threatening to end the relationship.

The IA, not wanting to be abandoned, suddenly starts to do recovery work. They take their partner out on dates, start to share emotions, spend more quality time, etc. In other words, they start doing everything their partner has been asking for all along. As a result, the partner begins to feel safe and loved. They stop threatening to leave the relationship.

The IA, sensing that the danger of abandonment has passed, gradually stops putting in the effort. Things go back to the way they were. The emotional distance is comfortable for the IA, so they are satisfied. The partner is not. The cycle starts all over again. This is highly emotionally damaging to a partner. There are only so many cycles that a partner can stand before they exit the relationship permanently.

The sad thing is that the stabilization cycle has nothing to do with the IA helping their partner heal. It has everything to do with making the relationship less painful for themselves. Whether it's the avoidance of abandonment or simply getting tired of hearing their partner's complaints, the IA engaged in stabilization is making selfish choices when it comes to recovery.

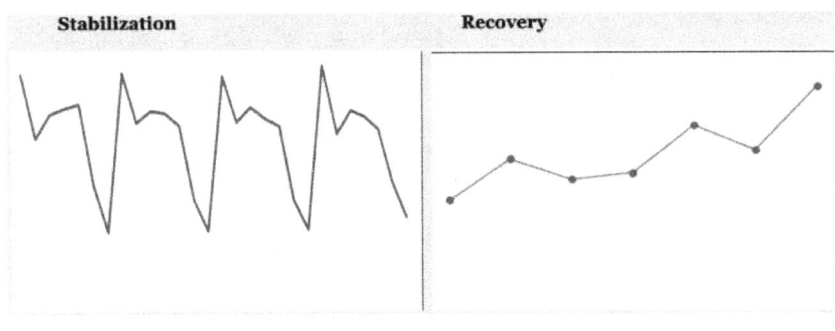

The two graphs represent the difference between stabilization and true recovery. If you look at the stabilization graph, you can see highs and lows. However, if you draw a line of best fit across the peaks of the graph, you can see that it's a flat line. The relationship is going nowhere. The "highs" only feel like progress because the lows hurt so much. The pain of emotional distance is only temporarily relieved, only to start all over again. This is not recovery.

If you look at the recovery graph, you can see that it looks quite different. Although highs and lows are represented on the graph, the line of best fit would show an upward trajectory. This graph represents consistent effort. Although there will be times when you aren't perfect (represented by the lows), you and your relationship will be making progress overall. This is true recovery.

HELPING MY PARTNER HEAL (PART 1)

How are you currently stabilizing your partner? If not, then what evidence do you have that you're in recovery?

When have you stabilized your relationship?

What needs did you meet for your partner that, once the relationship was stabilized, you stopped?

What did you prioritize over staying consistent in recovery?

> **Matthew 7:24-27 MSG** These words I speak to you are not incidental additions to your life, homeowner improvements to your standard of living. They are foundational words, words to build a life on. If you work these words into your life, you are like a smart carpenter who built his house on solid rock. Rain poured down, the river flooded, a tornado hit-but nothing moved that house. It was fixed to the rock. But if you just use my words in Bible studies and don't work them into your life, you are like a stupid carpenter who built his house on the sandy beach. When a storm rolled in and the waves came up, it collapsed like a house of cards.
>
> Father, Give me the grace to break the nature of selfishness that is so deeply rooted in my character. Help me to stay on the narrow path of righteousness every day and in every way. I want my house, my relationship with my partner, to be built on solid rock. When rain, storms, floods, or tornados hit, nothing will move because our relationship is built upon the Rock of Your Word! In Jesus' name, Amen.

Step 9 Connection: With being up and down about recovery, write a sentence Recognizing the Wrong, Understanding the Pain, and Taking Responsibility (RUT) for your lack of consistency.

R -

U -

T –

PARTNER CONNECT Explain this exercise to your partner. Ask them if they resonate with it. Ask them if they think you are still doing it. Take note of what they say so that you can identify ways to improve.

HELPING MY PARTNER HEAL (PART 1)

Emptying the Pain Closet   Exercise 37

We became the wounding partner through sexual betrayal and intimacy avoidance-related attitudes and behaviors. We have created many different sizes and intensities of pain for our partners, whom we call the wounded partner.

It's like our partners have this big pain closet and, in that closet, there are many different sizes of pain containers. Many of these pains, we created, and others we didn't. Regardless, our behavior has made all their pain harder to bear.

We must decide as the wounding partner to help our wounded partner to empty their pain closet.

How do we help them empty their pain closet? What do they need daily to feel safe enough to empty it?

Again, connected to standing shoulder to shoulder with our partners in their pain – as well as staying connected to hearing, validating, and empathizing with their pain – we must commit to helping them empty the pain closet. We must be intentional about it.

What will you do this week to help unpack a container of their pain?

Many times, men say that women never forget. I would challenge that. I'd say that there's a good chance that it's not that she doesn't want to forget, but she's never gotten the opportunity to process the pain that would allow her to let it go. We have found in our practice at Becoming Well that partners were able to process their pain containers, most of those containers go away and never come back.

Some pain containers are so hurtful on so many different levels that it takes a lot of time and effort and multiple conversations to process. But that deep pain container can be taken out of the closet.

> **Jeremiah 33:6 MSG** But now take another look. I'm going to give this city a thorough renovation, working a true healing inside and out. I'm going to show them life whole, life brimming with blessings. I'll restore everything that was lost to Judah and Jerusalem. I'll build everything back as good as new. I'll scrub them clean from the dirt they've done against me. I'll forgive everything they've done wrong, forgive all their rebellions. And Jerusalem will be a center of joy and praise and glory for all the countries on earth. They'll get reports on all the good I'm doing for her. They'll be in awe of the blessings I am pouring on her.

Father, do a thorough and complete renovation on our relationship. Work Your healing power so we can be whole. Restore what has been lost because it is Your desire that our relationship be filled with blessings. I call upon Your loving kindness and tender mercies and I thank You for it. In Jesus' name, Amen.

THE FOUNDATIONS OF RECOVERY - PART 1 GROUND ZERO

Step 9 Connection: Complete this statement as many times as they have pain containers:

"My partner has pain from_____ and I am responsible for _____ about that container."

PARTNER CONNECT To complete section one of the exercise, please ask your partner what would help them empty their pain closet and what they need from you to feel safe enough to share with you.

Empathy Exercise   Exercise 38

This is a combination of several communication tools, including Dr. Doug Weiss's understanding exercise, the speaker/listener exercise from the book *Fighting for your Marriage*, and other adaptations to increase the effectiveness of this extremely helpful tool.

<u>There are 6 steps to effectively using this tool with a couple of pre-steps.</u>

Step 0 – Self Regulate

Step 0 – Demeanor Check

<u>Step One: Get to the Heart of the Matter</u>

Step one will start with what we call a "**pain statement.**"

- The point of step one is that no matter the statement, your job is to get under it and **find the source of the pain**.
- **Don't Defend. Explain and correct.**
- Using the **speaker/listener technique**, let your partner talk.
  - **REMINDER**: You are using the speaker/listener technique ONE WAY. When using this exercise, it is not your turn.
  - *If you make it about you, you will undermine the whole experience.*

Speaker Rules:

1. Speak only for yourself
2. Be respectful
3. Keep your statements brief and to the point
4. Stop frequently to let the listener repeat what you said

Listener Rules:

1. Repeat what you heard by saying, "what I heard you say is _____. Is that correct?"
2. If you weren't correct with what you repeated, speaker should say "no" and say it again.
3. Keep repeating this process until you get what they said correctly.
4. Once you repeat what they said correctly, ask, "is there more?"
5. DO NOT rebut.

<u>Step Two (Part A): Discover and Explore Your Partner's Feelings</u>

- Once you have gotten to the heart of the matter, ask them to express how the situation has them feeling. You can ask questions such as, "how does that make you feel?" or "how do you feel about that?"
- **Hint: This is another place where it is useful to use the Speaker/Listener Technique to repeat what your partner has told you. This will make sure you understand what they are trying to say before moving on.**

Step Two (Part B):

- Once your partner has expressed their feelings, pause for a moment. Imagine a time when you felt similarly. What happened? How did it affect you? Did it have lasting effects?

Step Three: Validate Your Partner's Feelings

- "It makes sense that you could feel that way." This requires empathy. You're putting yourself in your partner's shoes and moving from your self-centered perspective to your partner's perspective.

If they are still escalating, you missed something and need to go back.

Step Four: Take Responsibility

In this step, there are only two acceptable responses:

1. "Yes, I did that." (If you did it, own it.)
2. "I don't know if I did that this time, but I definitely have done that in the past. I can see why you would think that I did it and feel the way you feel about it."

Step Five: Ask Your Partner What They Need

Ask your partner what they need from you. Remember, it's not helpful to evaluate what they need or interject with what you think they need or should need. Just accept it.

Step Six: Just Do It

List out at least 3 common pain statements where your partner is expressing deep pain, anger, and sadness about your actions/inactions.

1.
2.
3.

When your partner is in pain and expressing it to you, how do you feel?

Next to each feeling, what actions do you tend to take, almost without thinking about those actions?

What are the results of these actions/inactions? Name three scenarios below.

Feelings	Actions/Inactions	Results

> 1 Peter 3:8 MSG Summing up: Be agreeable, be sympathetic, be loving, be compassionate, be humble. That goes for all of you, no exceptions. No retaliation. No sharp-tongued sarcasm. Instead, bless-that's your job, to bless. Then you'll be a blessing and also get a blessing.
>
> Father, You know I need help in the area of empathy. This tool is designed to sharpen my empathy so that I can bless my partner. I ask that You grace me with Your supernatural help in this area and I thank You for it. In Jesus' name, Amen.

HELPING MY PARTNER HEAL (PART 1)

Use this page to track using the Empathy Exercise for the next 90 days.

Beneath each day, write the feeling your partner is having and why they are having it.

Day 1	16	31	46	61	76
2	17	32	47	62	77
3	18	33	48	63	78
4	19	34	49	64	79
5	20	35	50	65	80
6	21	36	51	66	81
7	22	37	52	67	82
8	23	38	53	68	83
9	24	39	54	69	84
10	25	40	55	70	85
11	26	41	56	71	86
12	27	42	57	72	87
13	28	43	58	73	88
14	29	44	59	74	89
15	30	45	60	75	90

THE FOUNDATIONS OF RECOVERY - PART 1 GROUND ZERO

Step 2 Connection: Do you believe a power greater than yourself can restore your relationship? Write a prayer below that can help you self-regulate. Check your demeanor from any time prior to hearing your partner's pain, or even from in the middle of hearing their pain.

PARTNER CONNECT As instructed in the exercise, please practice the Empathy Exercise with your partner for the next 90 days. Be sure to track your progress.

No Defend Challenge – 13 Weeks

Exercise 39

For the next 13 weeks, keep track each day of whether you defended, explained, or corrected your partner in conversation or conflict. Each day you do, your consequence will be 25 push-ups*.

Choose to use the **empathy exercise** instead. Keep track as well!

Week 1	M	T	W	T	F	S	S
Defend/Explain							
25 Push-Ups							
Understanding Exercise							

Week 2	M	T	W	T	F	S	S
Defend/Explain							
25 Push-Ups							
Understanding Exercise							

Week 3	M	T	W	T	F	S	S
Defend/Explain							
25 Push-Ups							
Understanding Exercise							

Week 4	M	T	W	T	F	S	S
Defend/Explain							
25 Push-Ups							
Understanding Exercise							

Week 5	M	T	W	T	F	S	S
Defend/Explain							
25 Push-Ups							
Understanding Exercise							

Week 6	M	T	W	T	F	S	S
Defend/Explain							
25 Push-Ups							
Understanding Exercise							

Week 7	M	T	W	T	F	S	S
Defend/Explain							
25 Push-Ups							
Understanding Exercise							

Week 8	M	T	W	T	F	S	S
Defend/Explain							
25 Push-Ups							
Understanding Exercise							

Week 9	M	T	W	T	F	S	S
Defend/Explain							
25 Push-Ups							
Understanding Exercise							

Week 10	M	T	W	T	F	S	S
Defend/Explain							
25 Push-Ups							
Understanding Exercise							

Week 11	M	T	W	T	F	S	S
Defend/Explain							
25 Push-Ups							
Understanding Exercise							

Week 12	M	T	W	T	F	S	S
Defend/Explain							
25 Push-Ups							
Understanding Exercise							

PARTNER CONNECT As you track your progress, make sure to ask your partner daily if they experienced you defending yourself, explaining your side, or correcting them in conversation.

Week 13	M	T	W	T	F	S	S
Defend/Explain							
25 Push-Ups							
Understanding Exercise							

After 13 Weeks

Total times I defended: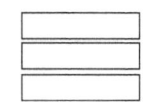
Total Push-ups Completed:
Total times I Understood:

*If you are unable to perform a push-up then:

a. Perform half push-ups
b. Or for health reasons, consider an alternative consequence that involves physical exertion.

> **1 Peter 3:8 MSG Summing up: Proverbs 14:12 AMP There is a way which seems right to a man and appears straight before him, but its end is the way of death.**
>
> Father, defending seems like the way I ought to go, but it always ends up very badly. It really is the way of death and especially the death of trust. Give me the grace to be honest in the kindest possible way. Help me to think outside myself and heal my partner's heart. In Jesus' name, Amen.

Daily Check In

Exercise 40

The next two pages are to be used on a daily basis as options for checking in with your partner. Use these pages as a guide for both of you. Agree ahead of time to follow these steps to the best of your ability. Over time, after you've had enough practice, work towards sharing without having these pages as a guide. Choose one, FANOS or Safer Check-In, to see which fits your relationship needs.

"FANOS" Check In

Here is a quick look at what FANOS is. Each letter is an aspect of your inner life that you will share with your significant other.

- **F**eelings: Share an emotion you experienced today. Use a list of feelings or The Feelings Wheel at first as you build an emotional vocabulary.
- **A**ffirmations/**A**ppreciations: This is a positive word for your partner for who he/she is. Tell him/her something you appreciate that he/she has done today.

This is "you are _____" and "I appreciated it when you _____."

- **N**eeds: Tell your partner something you need from him/her. This could be a need you just recognized or one you have mentioned before that still has not been met. Don't skip this one. Sometimes you may have to think for a minute before you can verbalize what you need.
- **O**wnership: What have you done wrong that you need to take ownership of? This can be one of the most healing and connecting points.
- **S**truggles/**S**obriety: Agree together beforehand on what struggle/sobriety topic each person will discuss. It can be any number of things. Some examples are your sobriety date, recovery work, your diet, exercise, raging, perfectionism, criticizing, compulsively checking up on your partner, or defensiveness. If you are an addict, you need to focus on sobriety and recovery work.

When sharing FANOS:

- One person goes through the entire FANOS, and then the other person goes through the entire FANOS.
- Talking through the entire FANOS should take no longer than two minutes. You do have time to do this! I don't care how tired you think you are, you have four minutes to connect with your significant other.
- When you listen to FANOS, your role is not to give feedback or fix. Your role is simply to listen and be present. This is an important opportunity to share safety and love.
- If you want to respond to something your partner said in his/her FANOS, wait until the next day. Actually, responding the next day can be a good sign that you were listening, you have been thinking about it, and you care about what was shared.

Here is an example FANOS:

- **F**eelings: I'm a little scared but hopeful about what is going on with our children. I feel overwhelmed by work and the kids' schedule. I feel determined to finish the project in the yard this weekend. I felt relaxed today when we were watching a movie together.
- **A**ffirmation/**A**ppreciation: I appreciate that you took out the trash like you said you would. Thank you for putting gas in the car and always keeping the car fueled.

- **N**eeds: I need for us to have more time together, like the time we spent on the couch tonight watching the movie.
- **O**wnership: I own that I did speak angrily to you when you asked me to go to the store. You did not deserve that and I apologize for that.
- **S**truggles/**S**obriety: I felt a tug to be defensive today when you told me that you wanted me to do the laundry, but I checked myself at the time.

REMEMBER, this is NOT a time to give feedback, criticize, correct, or shame one another. Simply listen to each other and know that the goal of this exercise is to build intimacy and restore trust. The key to this sharing time is to create safety while demonstrating connectedness, accountability, and acceptance.

HELPING MY PARTNER HEAL (PART 1)

The "SAFER" Check-In

©2016, Jacob Porter, Daring Ventures

Regular Communication to Rebuild Trust

Wounding Partner	Wounded Partner
Sobriety: "My sobriety date is….."	Safety: "My safety level today is…." (Provide a number between 0 and 10)
Accountability: "I want to apologize for when…"	Acknowledge: "I felt safest this week when…"
Feelings: "This week, the emotions I felt most were…"	Feelings: "This week, the emotions I felt most were…"
Express: "I've been learning about myself…."	Express: "I had the hardest time this week when…"
Recovery: "For my recovery, I have…and plan to…"	Requests: "You can help me feel safer by…"

Instructions for completing the SAFER Check-In

1. Set a designated weekly time and place for the check-in. Try to choose a time when you will be uninterrupted and not too tired.
2. Plan ahead for check-in. Be prepared with what you are going to say. Preparation can greatly enhance the experience by making it more thoughtful and meaningful.
3. Decide whether the wounding or wounded partner will share first. The first person will share their complete check-in. Then the second person will share their complete check-in.
4. While each person shares their check-in, the other person should try to use good talking and listening boundaries if they respond.
5. Remember, this process involves 2 traumatized people being vulnerable. Be gentle with yourselves and take a break before you come back to discuss any content/concerns in detail.

Step 2 Connection: Make a choice today to believe that your relationship can be repaired. With the help of God, all things are possible. With your partner, choose to believe, and ask for help with any unbelief you may have. In the space below, write a prayer about this desire to want to believe.

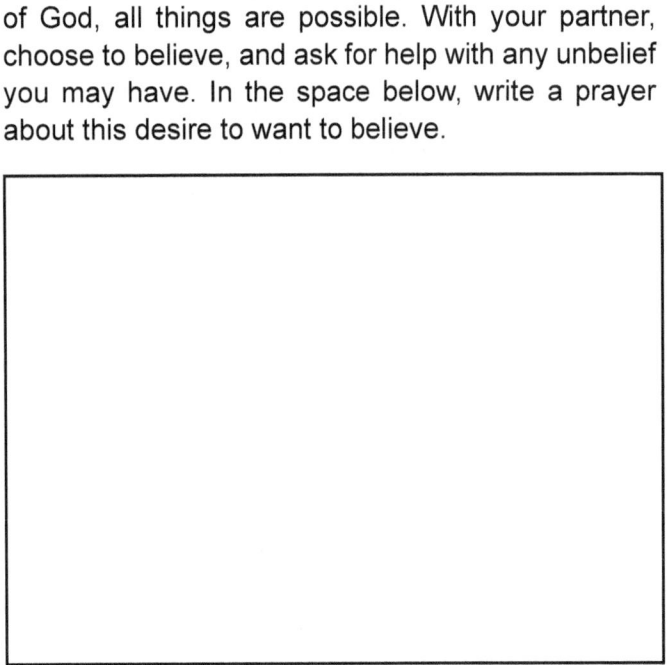

*** Close every day of daily check in with your partner with prayer. If you need a helpful acronym to P.R.A.Y., then be sure to P = Praise the good, R = Respond to challenges, A = Ask for help, and Y = Yield to the will of God

Ephesians 5: 25-28 MSG Husbands, go all out in your love for your wives, exactly as Christ did for the church- a love marked by giving, not getting. Christ's love makes the church whole. His words evoke her beauty. Everything he does and says is designed to bring out the best of her, dressing her in dazzling white silk, radiant with holiness. And that is how husbands ought to love their wives. They're really doing themselves a favor- since they're already "one" in marriage.

Father, I will check in with my partner on a daily basis. I will discuss and share my feelings, affirmations, appreciations, and needs. I will listen to their feelings, affirmations, appreciations, and needs. This is a two-way street, and I will be an excellent steward of my relationship with my partner. In Jesus' name, Amen.

<u>PARTNER CONNECT</u> If you haven't done so already, talk with your partner and arrange a daily time that works for both of you to do the check in.

Feeling Wheel

Exercise 41

"You got to Feel it to Heal it."

There are many exercises in this book that will require you to access where you or your partner lands on the wheel. We all fluctuate around the wheel throughout the day.

Treat this tool as a bullseye and apply it in two ways:

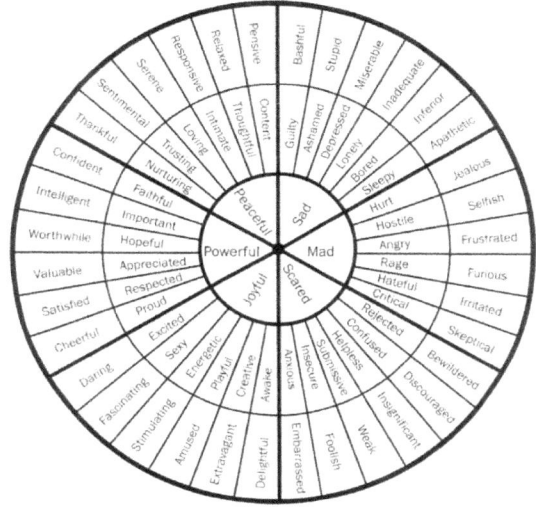

1. Identify your own feelings, starting in the middle-to-outer parts of the circle. Then, work toward the inward primary emotion. You can say something like:

   "I feel scared...really anxious about today."

2. Hear the feelings of others, namely your partner. First, they share what they are thinking or experiencing. Then, ask what feeling(s) are connected to that for them. Allow them space to get to the center of the wheel.

In your recovery from SA and/or IA, your ability to access your feelings can help identify what leads you into unhealthy thinking and/or lust.

See Appendix

In the next week, identify 2 feelings per day. Also, identify if you would have coped with these feelings with either sexual addiction or intimacy avoidant behavior.

Day	Feelings	Reason for feeling OR "I'd act out in _____ (SA/PA/IA) to cope"
1		
2		
3		
4		
5		
6		
7		

Jeremiah 33:6 ESV Behold, I will bring to it health and healing, and I will heal them and reveal to them an abundance of prosperity and security.

Father, as my partner and I use the tool of the feeling wheel, I ask that You honor this exercise. Reveal to us the very important feelings and situations that need to be dealt with so we may be healed and whole. In Jesus' name, Amen.

THE FOUNDATIONS OF RECOVERY - PART 1 GROUND ZERO

Step 3 Connection: Turning your will over to God is a daily process. This involves letting go of your will and trusting in God's will for your life. This is done with every feeling and desire of your heart. Write 3 statements of surrender for feelings you recorded above.

> Ex: "Lord, I surrender this feeling of _____ to you. I ask that your will be done, not my own, and that you will reveal what it is I need to find in you, not in my fleshly destructive coping mechanisms."
>
> 1.
> 2.

PARTNER CONNECT For the next 30 days, ask your partner to identify a feeling from the Feelings Wheel that they are experiencing and share it with you. Listen to what they have to say. Ask them to share what they are experiencing that contributed to their feeling.

HELPING MY PARTNER HEAL (PART 1)

Most Flawed Moment   Exercise 42

Sharing your daily flawed moments creates vulnerability and a deeper emotional connection with your partner.

We who are sexually addicted or intimacy avoidant put ourselves in the "good box" or "bad box." We think in black and white when it comes to being lovable, and while we all have flawed moments, the point of this exercise is to realize that you are still loveable even when you make a mistake.

Examples of what to share for Flawed Moments: Expressing anger towards a child or being defensive towards your partner

Examples of what to <u>not</u> to share for Flawed Moments: Driving over a curb or stubbing a toe

It's about getting vulnerable. We share the week's most flawed moment in recovery groups in order to experience acceptance even though we make mistakes.

Have your actions caused you to feel broken or ashamed? List specific ones here and share them with a sponsor or recovery partner.

If your partner is open to it, practice sharing your flawed moment accompanied with acceptance for a week.

	Day 1	Day 2	Day 3	Day 4	Day 5	Day 6	Day 7
Flawed Moment							

When your partner shares their flawed moment respond with

"Thank you for telling me, I still love you."

> **Philippians 3:12-14 MSG** I'm not saying that I have this altogether, that I have it made. But I am well on my way, reaching out for Christ, who has so wondrously reached out for me. Friend, don't get me wrong: By no means do I count myself an expert in all of this, but I've got my eye on the goal, where God is beckoning us onward-to Jesus. I'm off and running, and I'm not turning back.
>
> Father, I will share my flawed moments with my group and my partner. I want to be vulnerable and have a deeper emotional connection with my partner. I want to have a deeper and more emotional connection with You, too. In Jesus' name, Amen.

Step 2 Connection: Belief in God means that we are fully known and accepted. Do you believe that about yourself? Why? If not, what characteristic(s) of God opposes being known and accepted regardless of our flawed moments?

PARTNER CONNECT Ask your partner if they are open to doing this exercise with you. If they are, practice it every day with them.

Maintain a Sobriety Focus

Staying Sober Checklist — Exercise 43

This exercise is specifically for the sexually addicted who need to reflect on their actions pertaining to a relapse from sobriety. Your addict mind will try to bend boundaries, make excuses, and lie (to name a few) in order to return to lust and fantasy. Space is provided for you to reflect on anything else related to your relapsing. The point of this exercise is to self-evaluate and get back into the game of recovery. You are worth it!

	Yes	No	What I Plan to Do About It?
I stopped wearing my rubber band			
I played the victim, not taking 100% responsibility for my recovery			
I haven't made daily recovery calls			
I used electronic devices with no accountability software or blockers on them			
I haven't done the daily connecting exercises with my partner 6/7 times in the week			
I was lying prior to breaking sobriety			
I avoided intimacy with my partner prior to breaking sobriety			
I have stopped engaging my partner with the weekly check-in			
I have been grooming or flirting			
I have been objectifying others			
I have had fantasy thoughts that I ruminate on without taking them captive and telling others in recovery			
I haven't done my gratitude's 6/7 times in the week			
I haven't been consistently doing Book Work			

James 1:2-4 ESV Count it all joy, my brothers, when you meet trials of various kinds, for you know that the testing of your faith produces steadfastness. And let steadfastness have its full effect, that you may be perfect and complete, lacking in nothing.

Father, I will reflect on all my decisions that pertain to relapse of sobriety. I will hold myself accountable to You and to my counselors and group and partner to remain sober. I will keep all my requirements and not take the way of least resistance. The cost is way too high. In Jesus' name, Amen.

THE FOUNDATIONS OF RECOVERY - PART 1 GROUND ZERO

Step 3 Connection: Return to placing your will and trust in God. No matter what you plan to do, let God into your heart to give you the power and desire to choose recovery. Write a prayer highlighting this step with regards to your break of sobriety.

PARTNER CONNECT Share at least 2 areas that you have identified for improvement with your partner. What is your plan for change? What are you going to do to be accountable for making these changes?

3 Circles

Exercise 44

The 3 circles represent the areas of recovery all our actions fall into.

Inner Circle:

These are the actions we consider as "acting out" in either sexual addiction or intimacy avoidance.

Middle Circle:

These are the situations, breaking of boundaries, or actions done that may lead to you acting out in your inner circle behavior. (Ex: see HALT BS exercise)

Outer Circle:

These are the healthy behaviors that you do on a day-to-day basis. Using recovery tools, engaging with your partner, and maintaining a healthy self all belong here.

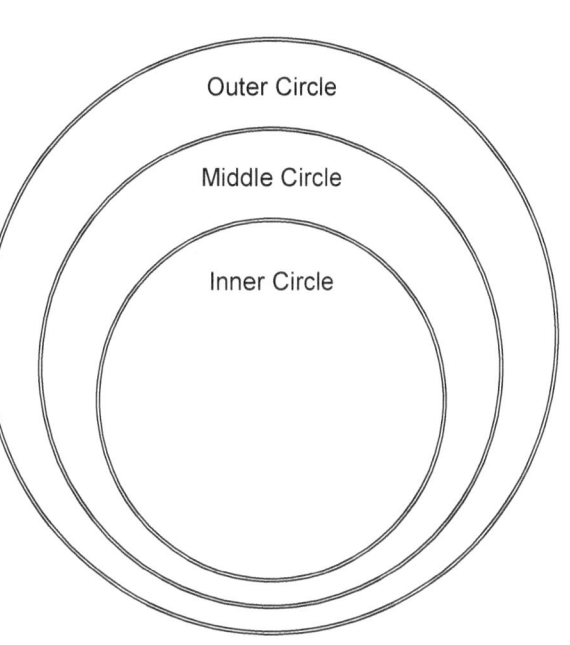

In the table below, identify 4 behaviors for each circle and the consequences of those actions for yourself and your partner. Consequences are how it affects or impacts you and your partner.

Inner Circle Behaviors	Consequences for Yourself	for Your Partner
1.		
2.		
3.		
4.		
Middle Circle Behaviors	Consequences for Yourself	for Your Partner
1.		
2.		
3.		
4.		
Outer Circle Behaviors	Consequences for Yourself	for Your Partner
1.		

**Psalm 19:7-9 CEB
The Lord's Instruction is perfect, reviving one's very being. The Lord's laws are faithful, making naive people wise. The Lord's regulations are right, gladdening the heart. The Lord's commands are pure, giving light to the eyes. Honoring the Lord is correct, lasting forever.**

Father, help me to identify and respond properly when I am in the middle or inner circle of these defined boundaries. Your ways will keep me safe, and my obedience will gladden Your heart. I only want to please You and love my partner. In Jesus' name, Amen.

THE FOUNDATIONS OF RECOVERY - PART 1 GROUND ZERO

2.		
3.		
4.		

Step 1 Connection: Share your behaviors and consequences with someone on a recovery call. You are not alone in this! We get better working with others in our recovery.

PARTNER CONNECT Share your inner, middle, and outer circle behaviors with your partner.

SA/PA Lapse and Relapse Worksheet

Exercise 45

Here, we return to the underlying heart issues that can very easily send you back into your sexual addiction coping strategies. This is your story. Your mind will always have tattooed into it the images of fantasy and feelings, but they could never be satisfied. In completing this exercise, you will be able to tell the story of your broken heart and mind and how you can now be freed daily from it.

Instructions: Answer the following questions to help you figure out what led you to your Sexual Addiction (SA)/Pornography Addiction (PA) behavior.

Describe the main reason you used pornography or behaved in a sexually inappropriate way.

Describe the inner thoughts and feelings that triggered your need or desire to use pornography or act out sexually.

Describe any external circumstances that triggered your need or desire to use pornography or act out sexually.

Think back to when this started. Describe the first decision you made (or remember making) that started the lapse or relapse process.

> **1 John 3:4 AMP Everyone who practices sin also practices lawlessness; and sin is lawlessness [ignoring God's Law by action or neglect or by tolerating wrongdoing- being unrestrained by His command and His will].**
>
> Father, Your word tells me to never look upon a woman with lust. The moment I allow my mind to wander is the moment I relapse. I have practiced lawlessness all my life. I have ignored Your law with my actions, by my neglect, and by my tolerance of wrongdoing. I now consecrate my mind and my heart to You. I will submit to Your laws and Your ways. I will never again tolerate wrongdoing but will practice restraint against it. I am the righteousness of God in Christ Jesus! In Jesus' name, Amen.

Step 10 Connection: Recovery is ongoing. Name a step, from Steps 1-9, that has been meaningful for your ongoing recovery from SA/PA and why.

PARTNER CONNECT If you have already confessed your SA and PA behavior to your partner, please share this exercise with them. Describe what you have learned about yourself.

Appreciation and Resignation Exercise 46 Letters for SA/PA/Infidelity

We begin this exercise by recognizing and appreciating what your sex addiction has provided for you. This is an important process of recovery because your perception of sex has been shaped by years of experiences. You resorted to acting out to soothe yourself, cope with life, feel powerful, feel loved, control satisfaction, be content, escape your circumstances, relive fantasy, and/or satiate your sexual desires.

Your connection to sex, whether acting out with others or yourself, has provided something for you. Recall those times when you held value for your sexual addiction. Even though it may have been momentary, what was the nature of appreciation you can name? Record at least 10.

1. _____
2. _____
3. _____
4. _____
5. _____
6. _____
7. _____
8. _____
9. _____
10. _____

Now, using these, write a letter to the sexual addiction as if it were a person standing in front of you, like a friend who has benefited you. Whether in your childhood or adulthood, the addiction gave you a sense of false control, happiness, satisfaction, and comfort.

Dear sex addiction,

Thank you for _____

_____

_____

_____

_____

_____

_____

_____

> **Romans 12:2 ESV Do not be conformed to this world, but be transformed by the renewal of your mind, that by testing you may discern what is the will of God, what is good and acceptable and perfect.**
>
> Father, I acknowledge my unholy past where I worshipped worthless idols. I thank You that I can now clearly see the harm and destruction that I caused to myself, my partner, my children, and my community. I repent and vow to only worship You and live according to Your holy ways. In Jesus' name, Amen.

THE FOUNDATIONS OF RECOVERY - PART 1 GROUND ZERO

Next, you will pair this appreciation with resignation.

MAINTAIN A SOBRIETY FOCUS

Resignation will be necessary for you to move on from the destruction that sex addiction has caused you. Think of how that friend of addiction has lied to, stolen from, tricked, and misguided you. Recognize the pain, grief, damage, and destruction the addiction has caused you, your relationships, and your children. Look addiction in the eyes and choose to say goodbye. Resign from the fantasy and lies it has told you and choose to live in reality.

Think of at least 15 reasons to resign.

1._____
2._____
3._____
4._____
5._____
6._____
7._____
8._____
9._____
10._____
11._____
12._____
13._____
14._____
15._____

Now, this time using these 15 or more points of hurt and/or destruction above, write a letter to the sexual addiction, formally divorcing yourself and your life from this addiction that has cost so much.

Dear sexual addiction,

I resign. It's time for you to go.

_____
_____
_____
_____

Step 3 Connection: Write a prayer thanking God for His will, His way, and His power to face whatever comes, to cope with life the way He wants you to. Express a desperation and dependency upon God's will for your life.

PARTNER CONNECT Do not share this activity with your partner. They are not likely to appreciate hearing how your addiction has benefitted you, even if this is a reality. Understand that your addiction has hurt them and their experience with your recovery is very different than yours.

MAINTAIN A SOBRIETY FOCUS

SA/PA Relapse Chain Exercise 47

Instructions: The last link in the relapse chain represents your use of pornography or other sexually addicted behaviors. Each preceding link represents a specific relapse warning sign. Identify as many warning signs as you can. Then state how much time elapsed between the earliest warning sign and the first time you acted out again. Also, state how you felt about acting out, and how your partner felt.

SA/PA Behavior →

Matthew 24:45-51 MSG "Who here qualifies for the job of overseeing the kitchen? A person the Master can depend on to feed the workers on time each day. Someone the Master can drop in unannounced and always find him doing his job. A God-blessed man or woman, I tell you. It won't be long before the Master will put this person in charge of the whole operation. But if that person only looks out for himself, and the minute the Master is away does what he pleases- abusing the help and throwing drunken parties for his friends- the Master is going to show up when he least expects it, and it won't be pretty. He'll end up in the dump with the hypocrites, out in the cold shivering, teeth chattering."

Father, give me the wisdom and the courage to identify warning signs that my feet are running off Your path and towards a trap. I ask that You ping my conscience when I make excuses for wrong choices, so that I can turn away immediately from danger. In Jesus' name, Amen.

Time elapsed from early warning signs to behavior	How I felt about my behavior	How my partner felt about my behavior

Step 1 Connection: Name the warning signs that you are powerless over occurring. Then, name choices you use can manage or stop.

PARTNER CONNECT Please share with your partner the choices you identified as helpful in keeping you from relapsing.

SA/PA Relapse Prevention Plan

Exercise 48

Relapses can happen very quickly in isolation, and because of pride in your own effort and willpower. This is why it is so important to humble ourselves daily about our need to retrain our mind over time and to lean on one another for support. Below are lines to describe how you will prevent relapses, and consequences for yourself if you don't. Our lives are unmanageable in addiction. Make the necessary choices to heal and recover!

Coping Skills: List at least 3 activities or skills you can use to get your mind away from acting out sexually or using pornography.

1. _____
2. _____
3. _____

Social Support: List at least 3 people you can talk to who you know will give you the truth when you are thinking about acting out.

1. _____
2. _____
3. _____

Consequences: In the left-hand column, list 4 consequences to your life if you continue to act out. In the right-hand column, list 4 benefits to your life if you remain sober from sex and/or pornography addiction.

Relapse Outcomes	Sobriety Outcomes

In addition to your own consequences, list at least 3 ways that your relapse would negatively affect your partner. If you're having trouble, ask your partner.

1. _____
2. _____
3. _____

> **Ephesians 5:29-33 MSG** No one abuses his own body, does he? No, he feeds and pampers it. That's how Christ treats us, the church, since we are part of his body. And this is why a man leaves his father and mother and cherishes his wife. No longer two, they become "one flesh." This is a huge mystery, and I don't pretend to understand it all. What is clearest to me is the way Christ treats the church. And this provides a good picture of how each husband is to treat his wife, loving himself and loving her, and how each wife is to honor her husband.
>
> Father, I choose not to be intimacy avoidant. You are intimate with me, and I choose to be intimate with You and my partner. I will treat my partner with the same love, respect, honor, and transparency that I would want to be treated with. I will share myself with You and with my partner. In Jesus' name, Amen.

Step 3 Connection: Write a prayer expressing your trust in God for the strength and determination to obediently follow this plan. Sit in silence with Him for 5 minutes, opening your heart to His will for your life.

Reflect on the experience here.

[ ]

PARTNER CONNECT If you have already confessed your SA and PA behavior to your partner, please share this exercise with them. Describe what you have learned about yourself.

MAINTAIN A SOBRIETY FOCUS

Top 5 Intimacy Avoidance   Exercise 49

Out of the list of 40 intimacy avoidant behaviors or ways of thinking, mark your top 20 ways of avoidance in relationships. Then, have your partner mark the top 20.

Lack of Empathy	Sexual Gratification Outside of Relationship	Easily Offended	Frequent Lying	Feelings are Facts	Emotionally Disengaged	Defensive	Sexually Avoidant
Self-Preoccupied	Constant Activity	Sabotages Emotional Connection	Blame-Shifting	Cynical Script	Poor Demeanor	All-or-Nothing Thinking	Avoid taking Responsibility
Stonewalling	Plays the Victim	Oversensitive to Criticism	Doing it My Way	Hero to Zero	Focuses on Faults of Others	Jumps to Conclusions	Contempt for Self/Others
Labels Themselves and Others	Requires Hoop Jumping	Prideful or Unteachable	Objectifies	Offends from a Victim Position	Suspicious of Partner	Reactive vs. Proactive in Relationship	Breadcrumbing or Love Bombing
Low Emotional Expression or Bandwidth	Inability to Handle Conflict Productively	Poor Self-Reflection	Gaslighting	Max or Min of Faults or Good Deeds	Spiritually Independent or Disengaged	Married but Unloved	An Intense Need to be Right

Now write out your top 10 based on these.

Lastly, with your partner, decide which 5 you will work on for the first 90 days and the second 90 days.

1st 90	2nd 90
1.	1.
2.	2.
3.	3.
4.	4.
5.	5.

Colossians 3:19 AMP Husbands, love your wives [with an affectionate, sympathetic, selfless love that always seeks the best for them] and do not be embittered or resentful toward them [because of the responsibilities of marriage].

Father, intimacy avoidance comes straight from the pit of hell. It is as detached and hateful as the devil is towards humankind. You are my Father, and I choose to be as attached and loving towards my partner as You are towards me. I choose to follow Your example for my life and will love my partner to the point of laying down my life for my partner. In Jesus' name, Amen.

THE FOUNDATIONS OF RECOVERY - PART 1 GROUND ZERO

Step 1 Connection: Recovery has choices. You will discover what you're powerless over and what you have the power to choose. Choose the date on a calendar, 180 days from now, when you will return to these top 10 and reassess, with your partner, which behaviors you are still showing.

I will revisit these top 10 with my partner on _____ (Date 180 days from now)
Signature_____

PARTNER CONNECT Ask for your partner's input to help you create your list of IA behaviors. Be sure to include your partner in all parts of this exercise. Share your commitment to revisit your top 10 with them. Remember, this is a contract between you and your partner. Failure to follow through on your part will hurt them more than they have already been hurt and will break their trust in your relationship.

Intimacy Avoidance – Appreciation and Resignation Letters

Exercise 50

Use the previous exercise - Top 5 IA

Express your appreciation and resignation to your ways of avoidant thinking and behaviors.
Go into detail about what you gained or got out of acting the way you do.
You will write 5 letters of appreciation and resignation, addressed to your behaviors.
Note: An extra appreciation and resignation page is provided for a sixth letter.

> **Philippians 1:6 NIV I am sure of this, that he who began a good work in me will bring it to completion at the day of Jesus Christ.**
>
> Father, I will complete the task assigned to me and I will do it well and to Your glory. In Jesus' name, Amen.

I write this to express **appreciation** for _____. (intimacy avoidant behavior #1)

_____
_____
_____
_____
_____
_____
_____
_____
_____
_____
_____
_____
_____
_____
_____
_____
_____
_____
_____

THE FOUNDATIONS OF RECOVERY - PART 1 GROUND ZERO

I write this to **resign** from acting _____. (intimacy avoidant behavior #1)

_____
_____
_____
_____
_____
_____
_____
_____
_____
_____
_____
_____
_____
_____
_____
_____
_____
_____
_____
_____
_____
_____
_____
_____
_____
_____
_____
_____
_____
_____
_____
_____
_____
_____
_____
_____
_____
_____

I write this to **resign** from acting _____. (intimacy avoidant behavior #1)

MAINTAIN A SOBRIETY FOCUS

I write this to express **appreciation** for _____. (intimacy avoidant behavior #2)

THE FOUNDATIONS OF RECOVERY - PART 1 GROUND ZERO

I write this to **resign** from acting _____. (intimacy avoidant behavior #2)

_____

_____

_____

_____

_____

_____

_____

_____

_____

_____

_____

_____

_____

_____

_____

_____

_____

_____

_____

_____

_____

_____

_____

_____

_____

_____

_____

_____

_____

_____

_____

_____

_____

I write this to **resign** from acting _____. (intimacy avoidant behavior #2)

MAINTAIN A SOBRIETY FOCUS

I write this to express **appreciation** for _____. (intimacy avoidant behavior #3)

THE FOUNDATIONS OF RECOVERY - PART 1 GROUND ZERO

I write this to **resign** from acting _____. (intimacy avoidant behavior #3)

_____
_____
_____
_____
_____
_____
_____
_____
_____
_____
_____
_____
_____
_____
_____
_____
_____
_____
_____
_____
_____
_____
_____
_____
_____
_____
_____
_____
_____
_____
_____
_____

I write this to **resign** from acting _____. (intimacy avoidant behavior #3)

MAINTAIN A SOBRIETY FOCUS

I write this to express **appreciation** for _____. (intimacy avoidant behavior #4)

THE FOUNDATIONS OF RECOVERY - PART 1 GROUND ZERO

I write this to **resign** from acting _____. (intimacy avoidant behavior #4)

_____
_____
_____
_____
_____
_____
_____
_____
_____
_____
_____
_____
_____
_____
_____
_____
_____
_____
_____
_____
_____
_____
_____
_____
_____
_____
_____
_____
_____
_____
_____
_____

I write this to **resign** from acting _____. (intimacy avoidant behavior #4)

MAINTAIN A SOBRIETY FOCUS

I write this to express **appreciation** for _____. (intimacy avoidant behavior #5)

THE FOUNDATIONS OF RECOVERY - PART 1 GROUND ZERO

I write this to **resign** from acting _____. (intimacy avoidant behavior #5)

MAINTAIN A SOBRIETY FOCUS

I write this to express **appreciation** for _____. (intimacy avoidant behavior #6)

THE FOUNDATIONS OF RECOVERY - PART 1 GROUND ZERO

I write this to **resign** from acting _____. (intimacy avoidant behavior #6)

_____
_____
_____
_____
_____
_____
_____
_____
_____
_____
_____
_____
_____
_____
_____
_____
_____
_____
_____
_____
_____
_____
_____
_____
_____
_____
_____
_____
_____
_____
_____
_____
_____
_____

PARTNER CONNECT Do not share this activity with your partner. They are not likely to appreciate hearing how your IA has benefitted you, even if this is a reality. Understand that your behavior has deeply hurt them, and their experience with your recovery is very different than yours.

MAINTAIN A SOBRIETY FOCUS

IA Relapse Chain   Exercise 51

The last link in the relapse chain represents your use of IA behaviors. Each preceding link represents a specific relapse warning sign. Identify as many warning signs as you can. Then state how much time elapsed between the earliest warning sign and the first time you acted in an IA behavior again. Also, state how you felt about acting IA, and how your partner felt.

IA Behavior →

James 1:13-15 MSG Don't let anyone under pressure to give into evil say, "God is trying to trip me up." God is impervious to evil, and puts evil in no one's way. The temptation to give into evil comes from us and only us. We have no one to blame but the leering, seducing flare-up of our own lust. Lust gets pregnant, and has a baby: sin! Sin grows up to adulthood, and becomes a real killer.

Father, give me the grace to accurately identify every warning sign and weak link in my belief system and in my character. Give me the empathy for my partner to think about my partner's reaction when I come across each situation. I refuse to dishonor You or my partner in any way. In Jesus' name, Amen.

Time elapsed from early warning signs to behavior	How I felt about my behavior	How my partner felt about my behavior

Step 1 Connection: Name the warning signs that you are powerless over. Then, name choices you must use to manage your warning signs to cease from causing others pain with your avoidant behaviors.

PARTNER CONNECT Share what you wrote in Step 1 with your partner. What are the warning signs you have identified? What are the choices you can make to get yourself out of the relapse cycle?

Exercise 52   IA Relapse Prevention Plan

Coping Skills: List at least 3 activities or skills you can use to get your mind away from behaving in avoidant ways.

1. _____
2. _____
3. _____

Social Support: List at least 3 people who you can talk to that you know will give you the truth when you are thinking about avoiding your partner or any relationship.

1. _____
2. _____
3. _____

Consequences: In the left-hand column, list 4 consequences to your life if you continue to avoid intimate emotional relationships. In the right-hand column, list 4 benefits to your life if you are engaging in healthy mindsets and engaging in your closest relationships.

Relapse Outcomes	Relational Outcomes

Ephesians 5:29-33 MSG No one abuses his own body, does he? No, he feeds and pampers it. That's how Christ treats us, the church, since we are part of his body. And this is why a man leaves his father and mother and cherishes his wife. No longer two, they become "one flesh." This is a huge mystery, and I don't pretend to understand it all. What is clearest to me is the way Christ treats the church. And this provides a good picture of how each husband is to treat his wife, loving himself and loving her, and how each wife is to honor her husband.

Father, I choose not to be intimacy avoidant. You are intimate with me, and I choose to be intimate with You and my partner. I will treat my partner with the same love, respect, honor, and transparency that I would want to be treated with. I will share myself with You and with my partner. In Jesus' name, Amen.

MAINTAIN A SOBRIETY FOCUS

In addition to your own consequences, list at least 3 ways that your relapse into avoidant behaviors would negatively affect your partner. If you're having trouble, ask your partner how they feel and why.

1._____
2._____
3._____

Step 3 Connection: Write a prayer expressing your trust in God for the strength and determination to obediently follow this plan. Sit in silence with Him for 5 minutes, opening your heart to His will for your life. Name each of your intimacy avoidant behaviors in your silence with God. Reflect on the experience here.

PARTNER CONNECT Share this activity in its entirety with your partner. Ask them if they can identify anything you have missed.

Parting Words

In closing, I would like to thank you for using this workbook. We hope that it was helpful to you. While I know the road is long and tough to navigate, I encourage you to keep pressing on. As Winston Churchill once said, "If you are going through hell, keep going." If you do the work, don't give in, and seek help along the way, I know you will find your way out of the painful circumstances in which you have found yourself. We wish you healing, comfort, peace, and wholeness in your recovery journey.

Addendum

Yearly Tracker

Use this tracker combined with the weekly check-in to keep track of your efforts in recovery for the next year

Month	Dr/ N/R	Present in Relationship	Rating of Relationship	# of Calls	Recovery Score /100	Month	Dr/ N/R	Present in Relationship	Rating of Relationship	# of Calls	Recovery Score /100
Jan	/ /	/ 10	/ 10		/ 100	July	/ /	/ 10	/ 10		/ 100
	/ /	/ 10	/ 10		/ 100		/ /	/ 10	/ 10		/ 100
	/ /	/ 10	/ 10		/ 100		/ /	/ 10	/ 10		/ 100
	/ /	/ 10	/ 10		/ 100		/ /	/ 10	/ 10		/ 100
	/ /	/ 10	/ 10		/ 100		/ /	/ 10	/ 10		/ 100
Feb	/ /	/ 10	/ 10		/ 100	Aug	/ /	/ 10	/ 10		/ 100
	/ /	/ 10	/ 10		/ 100		/ /	/ 10	/ 10		/ 100
	/ /	/ 10	/ 10		/ 100		/ /	/ 10	/ 10		/ 100
	/ /	/ 10	/ 10		/ 100		/ /	/ 10	/ 10		/ 100
	/ /	/ 10	/ 10		/ 100		/ /	/ 10	/ 10		/ 100
March	/ /	/ 10	/ 10		/ 100	Sept	/ /	/ 10	/ 10		/ 100
	/ /	/ 10	/ 10		/ 100		/ /	/ 10	/ 10		/ 100
	/ /	/ 10	/ 10		/ 100		/ /	/ 10	/ 10		/ 100
	/ /	/ 10	/ 10		/ 100		/ /	/ 10	/ 10		/ 100
	/ /	/ 10	/ 10		/ 100		/ /	/ 10	/ 10		/ 100
April	/ /	/ 10	/ 10		/ 100	Oct	/ /	/ 10	/ 10		/ 100
	/ /	/ 10	/ 10		/ 100		/ /	/ 10	/ 10		/ 100
	/ /	/ 10	/ 10		/ 100		/ /	/ 10	/ 10		/ 100
	/ /	/ 10	/ 10		/ 100		/ /	/ 10	/ 10		/ 100
	/ /	/ 10	/ 10		/ 100		/ /	/ 10	/ 10		/ 100
May	/ /	/ 10	/ 10		/ 100	Nov	/ /	/ 10	/ 10		/ 100
	/ /	/ 10	/ 10		/ 100		/ /	/ 10	/ 10		/ 100
	/ /	/ 10	/ 10		/ 100		/ /	/ 10	/ 10		/ 100
	/ /	/ 10	/ 10		/ 100		/ /	/ 10	/ 10		/ 100
	/ /	/ 10	/ 10		/ 100		/ /	/ 10	/ 10		/ 100
June	/ /	/ 10	/ 10		/ 100	Dec	/ /	/ 10	/ 10		/ 100
	/ /	/ 10	/ 10		/ 100		/ /	/ 10	/ 10		/ 100
	/ /	/ 10	/ 10		/ 100		/ /	/ 10	/ 10		/ 100
	/ /	/ 10	/ 10		/ 100		/ /	/ 10	/ 10		/ 100
	/ /	/ 10	/ 10		/ 100		/ /	/ 10	/ 10		/ 100

Feeling Wheel

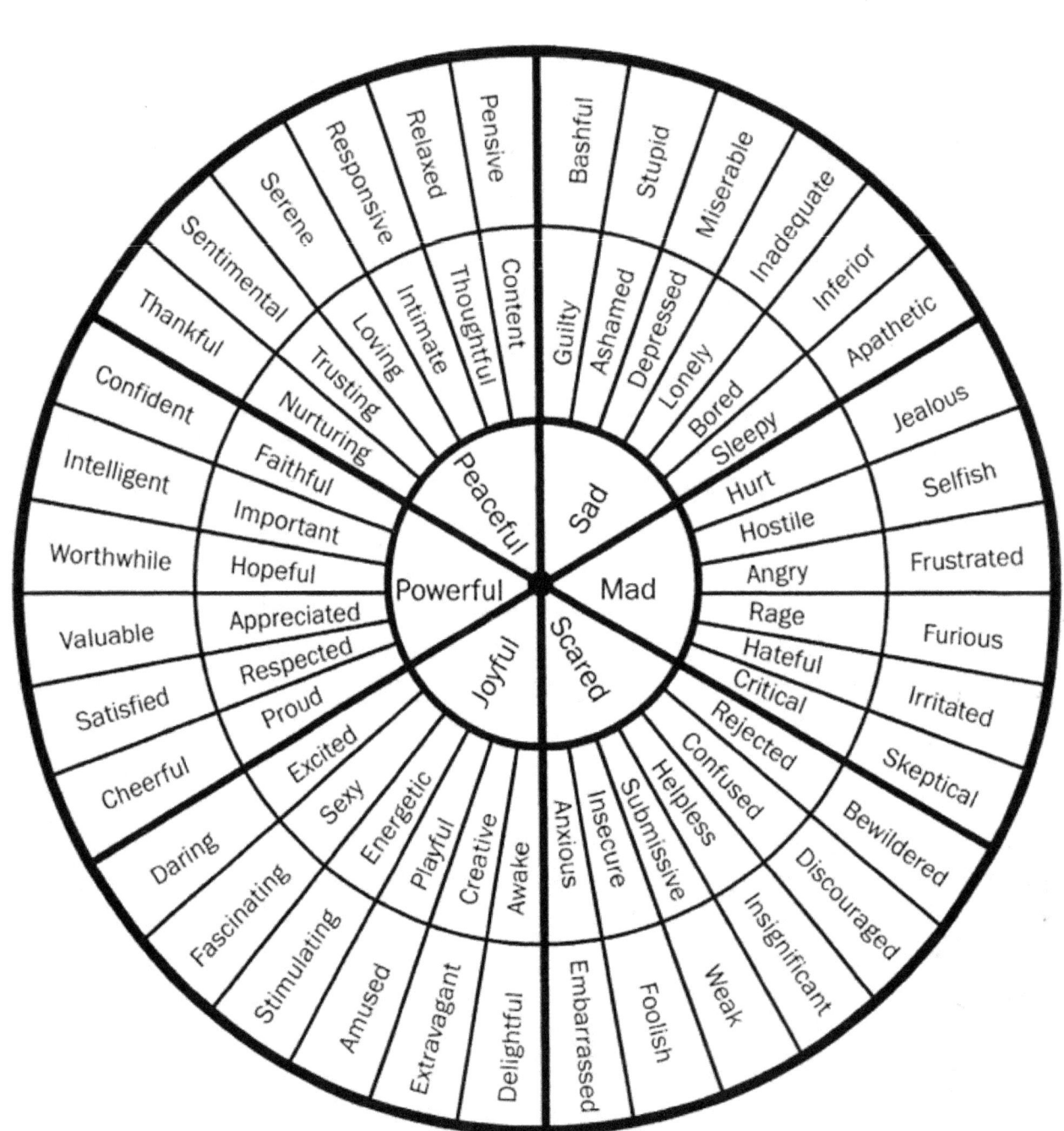

The Twelve Steps for Sexual Addiction

 1 We admitted we were powerless over lust and that our lives had become unmanageable

 2 We came to believe that a power greater than ourselves could restore us to sanity.

 3 We made a decision to turn our will and lives over to the care of our higher power as we understand them.

 4 We made a searching and fearless moral inventory of ourselves.

 5 We admitted to our higher power, to ourselves, and to others the exact nature of our wrongs.

 6 We were entirely ready to have our higher power remove all these defects of character.

 7 We humbly asked our higher power to remove our struggle.

 8 We made a list of all people we had harmed, and we became willing to make amends with them all.

 9 We made direct amends to whomever possible, except when to do so would injure them or others.

 10 We continue to take personal inventory and, when in the wrong, we promptly admit it.

 11 We seek through prayer and meditation to improve contact with our higher power, praying for knowledge of their will for our lives and the strength to carry it out.

 12 Having had a spiritual awakening from our experience through the steps, we seek to share with others and practice our principles in all our relationships.

The Twelve Steps for Intimacy Avoidance

 1 We admitted we were powerless over avoidance and that our lives had become unmanageable

 2 We came to believe that a power greater than ourselves could restore us to sanity.

 3 We made a decision to turn our will and lives over to the care of our higher power as we understand them.

 4 We made a searching and fearless moral inventory of ourselves.

 5 We admitted to our higher power, to ourselves, and to others the exact nature of our wrongs.

 6 We were entirely ready to have our higher power remove all these defects of character.

 7 We humbly asked our higher power to remove our struggle.

 8 We made a list of all people we had harmed, and we became willing to make amends with them all.

 9 We made direct amends to whomever possible, except when to do so would injure them or others.

 10 We continue to take personal inventory and, when in the wrong, we promptly admit it.

 11 We seek through prayer and meditation to improve contact with our higher power, praying for knowledge of their will for our lives and the strength to carry it out.

 12 Having had a spiritual awakening from our experience through the steps, we seek to share with others and practice our principles in all our relationships.

Recovery and 12 Step Prayers

Third Step Prayer (Page 63, AA Big Book)

God, I offer myself to Thee — to build with me and to do with me as Thou wilt. Relieve me of the bondage of self, that I may better do Thy will. Take away my difficulties, that victory over them may bear witness to those I would help of Thy Power, Thy Love, and Thy Way of life. May I do Thy will always!

Fourth Step Prayer (Page 67, AA Big Book)

This is a sick man. How can I be helpful to him? God, save me from being angry. Thy will be done.

Seventh Step Prayer (Page 76, AA Big Book)

My Creator, I am now willing that you should have all of me, good & bad. I pray that you now remove from me every single defect of character that stands in the way of my usefulness to you & my fellows. Grant me strength, as I go from here to do Your bidding. Amen.

Eighth Step Prayer (Page 76, AA Big Book)

Faith without works is dead.

Tenth Step Prayer (Page 85, AA Big Book)

How can I serve Thee? Thy will (not mine) be done.

Eleventh Step Prayer (Twelve Steps and Twelve Traditions, p. 99)

Lord, make me a channel of Thy peace – that where there is hatred, I may bring love – that where there is wrong, I may bring the spirit of forgiveness – that where there is discord, I may bring harmony – that where there is error, I may bring truth--that where there is doubt, I may bring faith--that where there is despair, I may bring hope – that where there are shadows, I may bring light – that where there is sadness, I may bring joy. Lord, grant that I may seek to comfort rather than to be comforted – to understand, than to be understood – to love, than to be loved. For it is by self-forgetting that one finds. It is by forgiving that one is forgiven. It is by dying that one awakens to eternal life. Amen

Serenity Prayer (Reinhold Niebuhr)

God, grant me the serenity to accept the things I cannot change,
The courage to change the things I can,
And the wisdom to know the difference.

40 ways to be IA
(Intimacy Avoidant)

1. **Marked lack of empathy.** Has trouble putting themselves in someone else's shoes. Often comes off as insensitive or uncaring. When others try to share their perspective, they often impose their own views on the situation without listening to the other person's view. Often has trouble understanding cause and effect - in other words, how their actions are contributing to the reactions of others.

2. **Oversensitivity to criticism or perceives criticism when there is none.** This may stem from a fear of rejection, poor self-esteem, or a generally negative view of others' intentions. Oversensitivity to criticism has been linked to negative childhood experiences such as harsh criticism from a parent or caregiver, rejection from peers, or having a parent with unrealistically high expectations. People who are oversensitive to criticism (real or perceived) often have negative cognitive biases that cause them to interpret information in a negative way.

3. **Low emotional expression and bandwidth.** Has an inability or unwillingness (oftentimes both) to express emotion. Emotional range is generally very small (2 or 3 emotions shared, usually some type of anger). The term "emotional bandwidth" refers to someone's ability to handle or engage in emotional stimuli, whether the stimulus is their own or someone else's.

4. **Jumps to conclusions.** Involves jumping to conclusions without having supporting facts. Mind-reading is when people randomly conclude that others are reacting negatively to them. Fortune-telling is assuming things are going to turn out badly and acting like those assumptions are already established facts.

5. **Contempt for self/others.** Contempt for self often comes across as shame and/or self-pity. Contempt for others comes out as grandiosity, belittling, or criticism.

6. **Sabotages emotional connectedness.** According to research studies, people who sabotage their relationships often have low self-esteem, difficulty trusting people (especially their partners), and a fear of commitment or being hurt, abandoned, or rejected.

7. **Reactive vs. Proactive in relationships.** This person appears ambivalent or disinterested in creating opportunities for ongoing, consistent connectedness. Major efforts to show love to their partner only come when the partner is fed up and entertaining the thought of ending the relationship. These efforts often fade away once the partner is reconnected to them, leading to an ongoing cycle that alternates between disinterest, emotional pain, and love-bombing.

8. **Spiritually independent or disengaged.** This person refuses to share any intimate details of their spirituality with their partner, often claiming that their spirituality is "private".

9. **Hoop jumping.** Often a feature of Intimacy Avoidant relationships, the IA will make their partner jump through a series of "hoops" to receive love. Much of this behavior is born out of entitlement. IAs often use this behavior as an excuse to withhold intimacy from their partner or criticize them for a "lack of performance."

10. **Defensiveness.** Defensive people often have issues of power and control. They often perceive confrontation and/or accountability as threats. The purpose of defensiveness is typically to protect a person from feeling hurt or shame. Defensiveness comes in many forms, including blame-shifting, silence, denial, and even self-pity.

11. **Prideful and/or Unteachable.** Typically, a person is masking feelings of low self-esteem and self-worth with pride. Pride is often a byproduct of feelings of inadequacy and vulnerability. Being "unteachable" can stem from pride, jealousy, stress, anxiety, or feelings of inadequacy.

12. **Blame-shifting.** People who blame-shift are often in denial about their level of personal responsibility. They often can't accept the fact that they may be at least partially responsible for a failure or mistake. Another reason for blame-shifting is to make the other person feel guilty or shamed, to silence them.

13. **Offended from victim position.** This takes place when a person decides that their role as victim gives them the right to lash out and/or hurt others. Pia Mellody and Terrence Real call this "retaliation." Intimacy Avoidant people often put themselves in the victim position through blame-shifting, shame, and self-pity. This makes it easier to justify bad behavior.

14. **Suspicious of partner.** There are many reasons IAs are suspicious of their partners. Common reasons include adverse childhood experiences that cause a general lack of trust toward others, depression and anxiety, and negative experiences in past relationships.

15. **Gaslighting.** Gaslighting is defined as psychological manipulation, typically over a prolonged period, that causes the victim to question their thoughts, feelings, memories, and perception of reality. Gaslighting typically involves lying but is not the same as lying. People often lie to escape consequences. Gaslighters lie to intentionally cause someone else to doubt themselves.

16. **Stonewalling/Punishing through anger.** Uses anger or silence to control the conversation. With silence, the partner eventually gives up, which is the intent. Anger is often used to intimidate, and punishing through anger is done purposely to teach the person a lesson and make them think twice about saying anything again. In either case, both are being used to silence someone.

17. **Frequent lying.** For IAs, lying often comes in the form of leaving out important information to avoid unwanted consequences. In some cases, habitual lying can be a sign of a more serious personality disorder.

18. **Avoids taking responsibility for actions.** This can be a result of emotional immaturity, denial, a refusal to be vulnerable, or an avoidance of intense feelings of remorse, guilt, and/or shame. In more serious cases, it can be because the person truly feels that accepting consequences is beneath them or does not have any understanding that their actions have consequences.

19. **Breadcrumbing or Love Bombing.** Breadcrumbing is a form of manipulation in which a person gives another person just enough attention and/or love to string them along. Love bombing often comes in the form of excessive flattery, attention, or gifts being used to lure someone to gain security for themselves.

20. **Emotionally disengaged.** This often stems from a deep fear of being ridiculed or rejected. An emotionally disengaged person may have learned from previous relationships that showing emotions made them vulnerable to negative consequences. Emotional disengagement is often developed in the family of origin when one or both parents failed to communicate their emotions or were uncomfortable with the emotions of others.

21. **Feelings are facts.** A person who treats feelings as facts often experiences emotions so intensely that they feel real. This typically stems from emotional immaturity. It's related to the cognitive distortion of emotional reasoning: "I feel it, so it must be true."

22. **Poor self-reflection.** Otherwise known as a lack of self-awareness. People with poor self-reflection are often intensely afraid of judgement and rejection from others. They keep themselves in a "protective bubble." This "bubble" makes it difficult for them to get in touch with their inner selves.

23. **Self-preoccupation.** This often stems from early childhood experiences of feeling rejected by others. They also could have been brought up to believe that they didn't have to consider the feelings of others. Trauma can also play a role because the person may have learned that they couldn't trust others, and this developed into self-preoccupation. Self-preoccupied people are generally emotionally immature.

24. **Labels themselves and others.** Related to the cognitive distortion of Labeling, which is a form of overgeneralization. It can also be related to perfectionism. For example, instead of being able to accept that they made a mistake, a person might label themselves a "loser." Instead of being understanding about the faults of others, they may label others "losers" or "idiots." Instead

of describing a situation realistically, labeling typically involves using inflammatory terms and language.

25. **Focuses on the faults of others.** Typically used as a defense mechanism in order to avoid feelings of guilt, shame, or inadequacy. It can also stem from entitlement when a person feels everyone else it at fault for them not getting what they want or feel they deserve.

26. **Objectification.** Treats their partner, others, and even themselves as objects. This extends far past sexual objectification or reducing someone to the sum of their body parts. Objectification also shows up as treating someone as if there is no need to be concerned about their experiences and/or feelings, a refusal to honor boundaries, treating people as if they were tools to be used for the IA to achieve their own goals, and treating someone as if they were easily replaced with someone else (a refusal to acknowledge someone's uniqueness).

27. **Poor demeanor.** Acts frequently disgruntled, angry, or irritated. Doesn't listen to their partner's feelings or discounts their experience. When asked to participate in the nurturing of the relationship, acts like it's a huge imposition. When asked to be accountable for past and/or present actions, responds with anger, blame, or pouting.

28. **Sexually disconnected or avoidant.** Doesn't make eye contact during sex or is mentally "checked out." Sex often feels empty and transactional to the partner. Also common is a complete/almost complete avoidance of sex. Couples that have sex 6 or fewer times per year are considered to have a "sexless" relationship.

29. **Sexual gratification outside of committed relationship.** This isn't always the case, but when it is it's typically due to an inability to connect with the partner. For most, this will be done through pornography and masturbation. For some, it will involve getting emotionally or sexually connected with a real person who is not their partner. Sexual addiction and attachment disorders are often underlying issues, especially with serial cheating.

30. **Inability to handle conflict productively.** For some, this will show up as conflict avoidance, stonewalling, and/or people-pleasing. For others, this will involve blame-shifting, denial, and overall defensiveness.

31. **All-or-nothing thinking (black-and-white thinking).** Seeing things in black and white without shades of gray. Tends to associate others and self into 2 categories: good and bad. Signs of all-or-nothing thinking include a tendency to use extreme terms when describing things, perfectionism, inability to see both good and bad in people and/or self, negative self-talk, and fear of trying new things.

32. **An intense need to be right.** Possible reasons for always needing to be right include insecurity, a need for control, a fear of failure, a competitive nature, and cognitive biases or distortions (such as all-or-nothing thinking) that make it difficult to consider alternate perspectives or admit it when wrong.

33. **Easily offended.** Often related to the cognitive distortion of personalization, which is assigning blame to oneself for circumstances out of one's control. Other reasons include unresolved psychological or emotional issues, a perception that their honor or personally held beliefs are being attacked, a generally negative emotional state, or the struggle to consider another's point of view.

34. **Maximization and minimization of faults and/or good deeds.** Tends to see others' faults as "huge" and their own as "not so bad." Tends to see their contributions as "huge" and others' contributions as minimal. In extreme cases, this can be due to grandiosity that contributes to a false sense of self-importance.

35. **Workaholism.** Many workaholics seek approval and become overly focused on work and "busyness" to gain approval and respect from others. Sometimes workaholism also occurs when the person is trying to avoid intimacy in their relationships.

36. **Plays the victim.** Playing the victim is a manipulative tactic. It is often used to avoid taking responsibility, gain sympathy and attention from others, and/or to discredit the experience and feelings of a person they have wronged.

37. **Hero or Zero.** Since IAs tend to see things in black and white without shades of gray, they tend to see themselves as a complete "hero" without faults or a "zero" with nothing but faults. This mentality often leads to blame-shifting, going "victim," and even complete denial of the issues.

38. **I did it my way.** This is an unwillingness to accept influence from their partner. IAs are typically highly independent and often don't listen to the suggestions of their partners when making decisions. Many partners define an IA partner as "an island."

39. **Cynical Script.** A bad story being played repeatedly in the person's head to excuse their poor treatment of the partner. The cynical script is often used to play the victim.

40. **Married but Unloved:** If married, the partner feels as if they are alone in it all. Many partners married to Intimacy Avoidants describe this as a surprise. It is common for Intimacy Avoidants to act differently before marriage than after marriage. Once the commitment to marriage is made, Intimacy Avoidants start to pull away from their partners in the ways that matter most. Partners may describe the relationship as sexless, devoid of intimacy, and disconnected.

Workgroups and Intensives

Men's Becoming Well Workgroups

Some guys have been in groups before; others have not. If you're committed to recovery from Sexual Addiction, Intimacy Avoidance, or Infidelity and are committed to rebuilding trust in your marriage, then our Men's Becoming Well Workgroups will be a good fit for you. Our men's groups focus on building and maintaining integrity, restoring intimacy in relationships, and rebuilding trust. They concentrate on two things: how to stop acting out and be accountable for the behavior that is breaking trust in the relationship, and how to develop the character and empathy it will take to support the relationship moving forward. And unlike many recovery groups out there, our guys are both finding sobriety and maintaining it.

Our groups are led by trained facilitators who have walked through many of these issues themselves, know how to stay sober, and know how to win in their relationship. The groups are small in size (no more than 8 people) so that each person can get the attention they need to address specific issues.

Each week, participants will hear a teaching from a trained professional and receive assignments and exercises that facilitate recovery for both themselves and their relationships. Participants will also have access to an online education portal, videos that explain the concepts talked about during group, and tutorials on how to work exercises and complete assignments.

Another thing that makes our groups different is that we welcome input from the wounded partners. Most programs exclude the partner, expecting that they stay in a relationship and take their partner's word for it that they're doing the work. When we hear from partners about past experiences, they often complain that nothing was shared with them, and they didn't even know what was going on most of the time.

Although we want to stress that the men need to own and work through their own recovery, and no partner can do that for them, we assign exercises to include the partner in rebuilding the relationship. Additionally, we offer a free monthly video conference call in which we update partners on what the guys will be working on that month and allow them to ask questions. Those meetings are typically led by Matt and Laura Burton personally.

Join a Men's Becoming Well workgroup today
www.BecomingWellInstitute.com

Men's Sexual Addiction, Infidelity & Intimacy Avoidance Recovery Intensives

Sexual addiction, infidelity, and intimacy avoidance can be isolating. Whether they're recovering from physical or emotional affairs, infidelity through pornography or other forms of sexual acting out, or intimacy avoidance, men entering recovery often feel like they are going it alone. Maximize your intensive experience by joining with other men to work through issues common to sexual addiction, infidelity, and intimacy avoidance. A Men's 3-Day Recovery Intensive can provide you with a safe environment to voice your pain and concerns, and to learn techniques for healing.

Intensives in a group format provide hope that you are not alone. You will hear the stories and struggles of others. You will also hear from Laura Burton, a trained and certified coach and a partner of someone who struggled with intimacy avoidance and pornography addiction. This will allow you to gain a deeper understanding of what both you and your partner are experiencing during this tough time in your relationship. You will not only see things through your relationship's historical lens, but through the eyes of others. This can help you gain a much-needed perspective that will help you move forward in recovery. Intensives focus on breaking the hold that addiction, infidelity, and intimacy avoidance have had on you and your partner. We partner with you to solve the issues that are holding you back from having the connection you have always wanted.

The Men's 3-Day Recovery Intensive offers daily group meetings and instruction by experts to ensure that the experience is tailored to you. Contact us today to schedule your intensive. Even if you are not currently in a relationship, the perspective you will gain throughout the intensive will help prepare you for the future—however that may look.

- Intensives are limited to 14 men per session.
- They take place at the Becoming Well Institute Intensive Center in sunny Tucson, Arizona.
- This includes an intake and assessment to identify your specific needs.
- We currently offer 2 distinct intensives for men: one with a focus on intimacy avoidance and one with a focus on sexual addiction and sexual/emotional infidelity.
- Each intensive is comprised of a combination of workgroups, group education, homework, exercises to work on with your partner, and personalized recovery plans.
- Contact us for pricing.

Our intensive center is located in beautiful, sunny Tucson, Arizona.

Learn more or sign up for a Men's Recovery Intensive today
www.BecomingWellInstitute.com

Sober Is Not Well
Men's "Going Deeper" Healing Intensives

Are you working on your recovery from porn/sexual addiction and intimacy avoidance? If so, why is your marriage still struggling so much and why do you still have behaviors and/or belief systems that are stunting you and your marriage from truly becoming well?

Why are you still stuck? Why aren't you getting a lot better? Why isn't your marriage getting a lot better? Because Sober is not Well. The areas underlying the SA and IA must be addressed. It's time to take another step in your recovery journey and focus on the roots.

In the Men's "Going Deeper" Healing Intensive, you'll focus on 4 specific areas of the 16 roots that slow or block recovery. These areas will be identified through a 2-part assessment process, one with you and the other getting your partner's input. You will spend your intensive time focused on the 4 identified focus areas in a process we call "Depth Work." That work will happen throughout the 3 ½-day intensive. The 16 root areas of potential intensive focus are:

Past Hurts Focus: Healing the injuries of your past to lessen their impact on you today and in the future.

o Trauma Focus; o Loss Focus; o Neglect Focus; o Abandonment Focus

Adaptive Behaviors Focus: Dismantling recurring struggles that are destroying you and/or your marriage and have you stuck.

o Other Addictions/Addiction Swapping Focus; o Anger Focus; o Specific Avoidance Focus; o Sexless Marriage Focus (Relational Sexual Avoidance); o Shame Focus; o Chronic Lying Focus; o Low or Lack of Empathy Focus; o Over Controlling of Self & Others' Focus; o Narcissistic Characteristics Focus; o Perpetual Victim Focus; o Emotional Immaturity Focus; o Chronic Negative Thinking Focus

The Details:

- Men's Healing Intensives are limited to 14 men per week.
- Healing Intensives take place on Thursday-Sunday.
- Your intensive will include intake assessment sessions to identify your particular needs.
- Each intensive weekend is comprised of groups, learning, processing, specific exercises, and personalized recovery plans.
- The time commitment per day is approximately 8 hours.
- Healing Intensive weekends are offered in-person only.

Our intensive center is located in beautiful, sunny Tucson, Arizona.
www.BecomingWellInstitute.com

Couple's Group Intensives
Moving couples from "Shattered to Strong"

Sexual addiction, infidelity, and intimacy avoidance can be isolating. Couples entering recovery often feel like they are going through it alone. Maximize your intensive experience by joining with other couples to work through issues common to infidelity and intimacy avoidance. A Couple's Group Intensive can provide you with a safe environment to voice your pain, concerns, and learn techniques for healing. Often, couples working through infidelity feel alone, judged, and hopeless. Intensives in a group format provide hope that you are not alone. You will hear the stories and struggles of others. This will allow you to gain a deeper understanding of what you and your partner are going through during this crisis. You will not only see things through your relationship's historical lens but also through the eyes of others. This can help you gain a much-needed perspective that will move you forward in recovery.

Group Intensive Weekends offer daily group meetings, instruction by experts, and individual sessions to help ensure that your experience is tailor-made for you. Couples leave feeling validated, understood, and hopeful— even if they were initially nervous about sharing their experience with others. Group Intensive Weekends will allow you to make connections with other people who understand what you are going through. This makes it possible for you to receive ongoing support through the relationships you form over the weekend. Couples will leave the Intensive with three distinct recovery plans: one for the wounding partner, one for the wounded partner, and one for the relationship.

- For couples who are in crisis after the recent discovery or disclosure of infidelity.
- For couples who are stuck and don't know how to get better.
- For couples who have experienced the isolation of infidelity, addiction, and intimacy avoidance and want to join a community of people who understand.
- For couples who want to learn from the experience of others in a safe environment.
- For couples who have done recovery work and want to deepen their experience.
- For couples who need a safe space to deal with what happened without feeling judged.
- For couples who want to hear from experts on how to recover from infidelity.
- For couples who want to accomplish in 3 days what normally takes 4-6 months.

The Details:

- Group Intensives take place in person on Thursday, Friday, and Saturday.
- Group Intensive Weekends include intake and assessment sessions to identify your specific needs.
- Each Group Intensive Weekend is comprised of a combination of workgroups, learning, homework, couple-specific exercises, and personalized recovery plans.
- The time commitment per day for Intensive Weekends is approximately 8-10 hours.

Learn more or sign up for a Couple's Group Intensive today
www.BecomingWellInstitute.com

Couples 7-Day: All In One Group Intensives

Are you a guy or married to a guy who's stuck or in a downward spiral, relationally or in your individual recovery, and who's unable to do what's needed/necessary to heal the shattered trust in your relationship?

What if you could experience all 4 intensives that Becoming Well Institute offers in a week? This means he could get the help he needs for his addiction and/or avoidance, as well as begin to heal the roots that created them. At the same time, she could begin to heal from a broken heart and shattered trust. You, as a couple, could begin to repair what has to date seemed impossible to heal.

Well, you can do all this through our 7-day All-In-One Intensive. At this intensive, the woman does key segments of the Women's Wounded Partner Intensive with other women also attending. The man does key segments of the Men's Recovery Intensive and Men's Going Even Deeper Intensive with the other men. Both partners work through key segments of the Couples Group intensive together, with the focus on helping couples navigate SA and IA recovery and Rebuilding Trust.

The four intensives that this all-in-one draws from:

- The Men's Recovery Intensive is for men striving to find lasting sobriety from porn addiction, sexual addiction, physical infidelity, emotional infidelity, intimacy avoidance, and/or sexual avoidance.
- The Wounded Partners Healing Intensive is for partners impacted by their wounding partner's sexual betrayal, intimacy avoidance, and/or sexual avoidance behaviors.
- The Men's "Going Deeper" Healing Intensives focus on the roots that created the addictive and destructive behaviors.
- The Couples Group Intensive helps couples understand what couple recovery looks like and what it takes to repair and rebuild the relationship, especially in the area of trust. It creates clarity and understanding of whether the wounding partner is serious about recovery and what the wounded partner should expect. It also creates a deeper understanding of what the benchmarks and timelines are for healing, all while supplying the tools and practice necessary to increase the likelihood for success.
- BONUS: Our All-In-One Intensive also teaches you how to help your School-Age and Adult Children Heal from the impacts of SA and IA.

For less than half of the total combined cost of all four intensives, you can experience them all. More importantly, you both benefit from the increased recovery & healing each intensive brings.

This is a great option for anyone wanting to accelerate the healing process, because intensives condense 4-6 months' worth of session work into 7 days.

Learn more or sign up for a Guys Group Intensive today
www.BecomingWellInstitute.com

Private Couple's Intensive

Moving couples from "Shattered to Strong"

Couples that attend Our One-on-One Private Couple's Intensives say it helps them understand and begin or advance the long journey of healing from the immediate and ongoing impacts of porn addiction, sexual addiction, infidelity &/or Intimacy avoidance - for both the Wounding and Wounded partner. We are able to take the time to deep-dive into what's specifically destroying the trust, individually and as a couple, and find the recovery you're desperately trying to either rediscover or discover for the first time.

For many couples, this intensive is their last stop before divorce court or a decision to stay permanent roommates. Couple after couple says that their time at the intensive allowed them to identify and begin the process of healing the hurt and devastation, as well as giving them a new relational system, as their current one just doesn't work for many reasons.

If you choose a Private Couple's Intensive, we will work with you to identify your specific needs to make sure your concerns are fully addressed in a private setting. Our Private Couple's Intensives are 3 days in length and will address both people in the relationship individually as well as the relationship itself.

Like the Guys Group Intensive, our Private Couple's Intensive is a great option for anyone wanting to accelerate the healing process, because intensives take 4-6 months' worth of session work and condense it into 3 days. You will receive an assessment of your unique issues, 7-8 hours per day of instruction, exercises and tools to help you move forward, and a personalized recovery plan for yourself and/or your relationship. We provide you a shame-free environment to address your specific issues.

And, if you choose a Private Couple's Intensive, we want you to know that partners are always treated with respect, compassion, and validation for the pain that their partner's issues have caused them. As a partner, you will never be blamed or asked to take any responsibility for your partner's choices. Also, if desired, we have full disclosure and polygraph services available.

Learn more or sign up for a Private Couple's Intensive today
www.BecomingWellInstitute.com

Books and Courses

Moving Couples from Shattered to Strong

REBUILDING TRUST

A Couple's Guide to Healing After Betrayal

MATT BURTON
LAURA BURTON

www.BecomingWellInstitute.com

Books and Courses

Moving Couples from Shattered to Strong

REBUILDING TRUST FOR CHRISTIANS

A Couple's Guide to Healing After Betrayal

MATT BURTON
LAURA BURTON

www.BecomingWellInstitute.com

Books and Courses

Moving Partners from Shattered to Strong

Mending After Betrayal

BOOK AND WORKBOOK

LAURA BURTON

www.BecomingWellInstitute.com

Books and Courses

Moving Partners from Shattered to Strong

Mending After Betrayal

BOOK AND WORKBOOK FOR CHRISTIANS

LAURA BURTON

www.BecomingWellInstitute.com

Books and Courses

Moving from Shattered to Strong

THE 12 STEPS TO BECOMING WELL

From Sexual Addiction

MATT BURTON
KEVIN ROSE

www.BecomingWellInstitute.com

Books and Courses

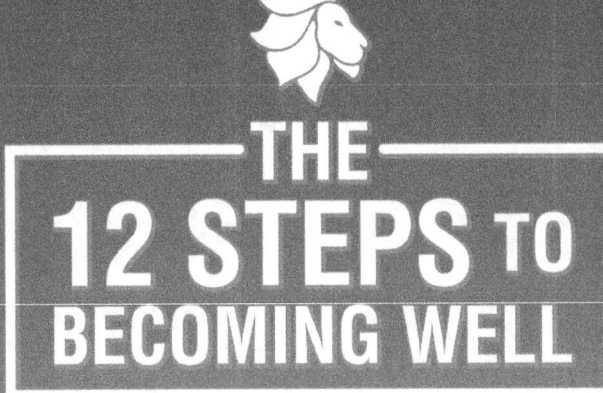

www.BecomingWellInstitute.com

Books and Courses

www.BecomingWellInstitute.com

Books and Courses

www.BecomingWellInstitute.com

Books and Courses

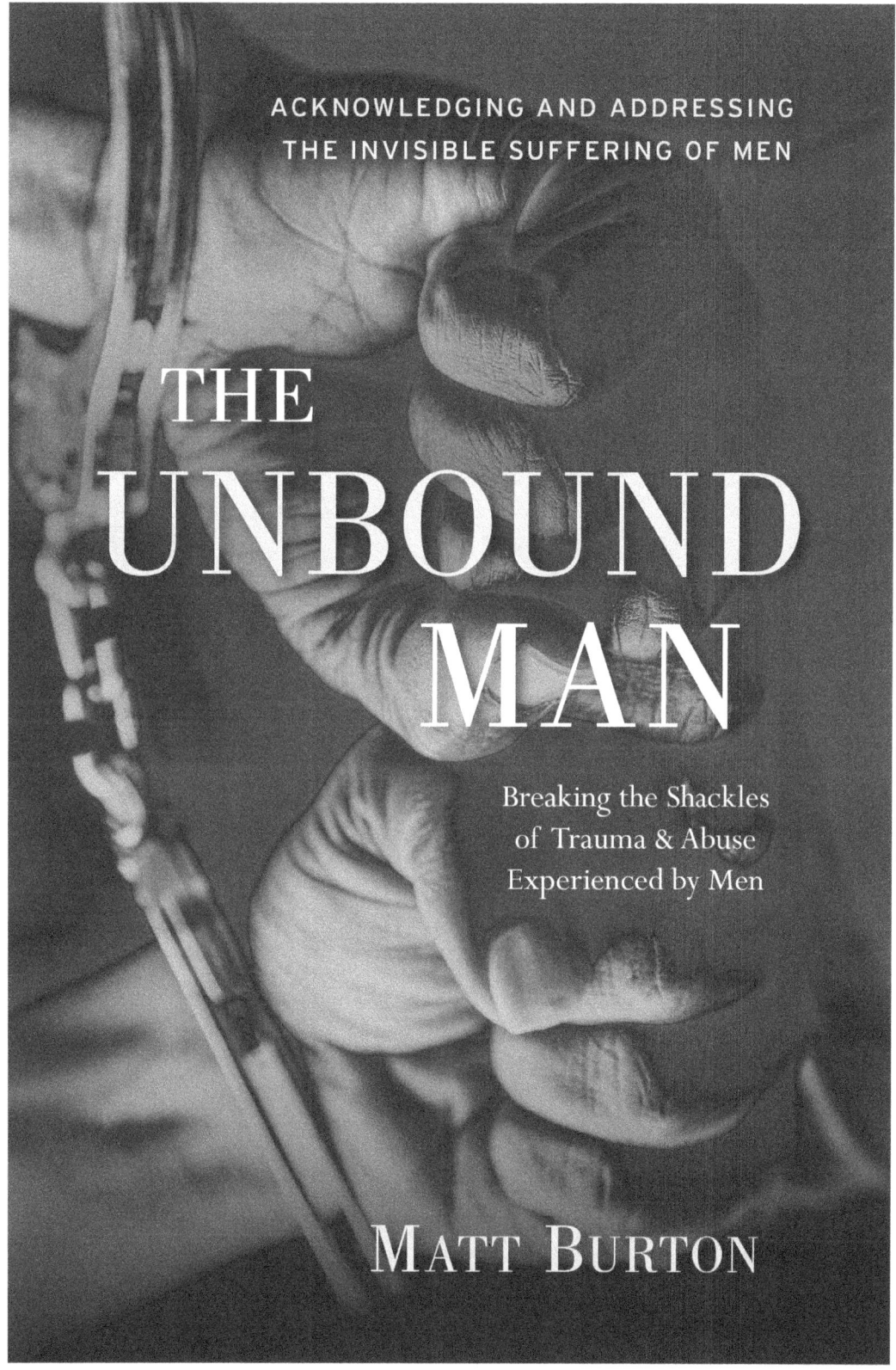

www.BecomingWellInstitute.com

Books and Courses

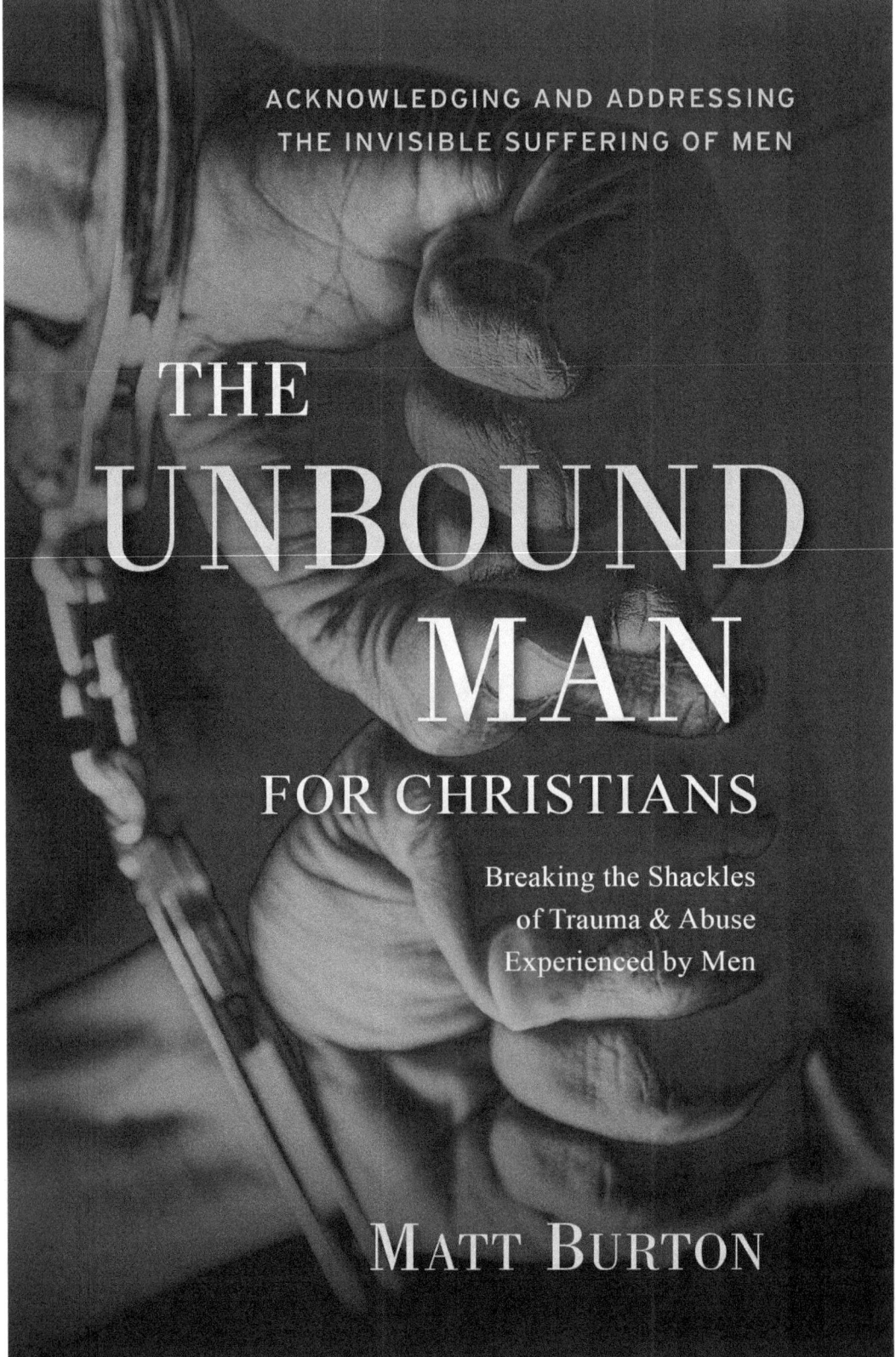

www.BecomingWellInstitute.com

Books and Courses

Books and Courses

Books and Courses

Books and Courses

Connect with Us

 www.facebook.com/mybecomingwell

 Becoming Well (@mybecomingwell)

 Becoming Well (@mybecomingwell)

 www.mybecomingwell.com

 info@mybecomingwell.com

 520-355-5322

www.ingramcontent.com/pod-product-compliance
Lightning Source LLC
LaVergne TN
LVHW081456060526
838201LV00057BA/3057